SENOIA BOY

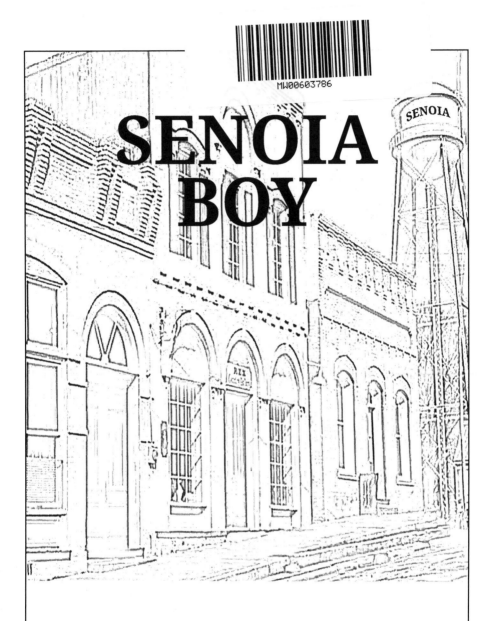

SENOIA

Ellis Crook
Edited by Angela McRae

Published in the United States of America.
Written by Ellis Crook.
Edited by Angela McRae.
Cover art by Deberah Williams.

ISBN # 978-0-578-69644-7

Contents

Foreword

by SAHS Board member & nephew, Hal Sewell

Most of us usually see Ellis Crook at his place of business. We've seen him there for many, many years – much like his father, Arry Lee Crook, before him. We therefore think of him as a businessman. In addition to his successful business operations, he is a family man and a man of faith. In addition to his immediate family, he has quietly provided assistance to other relatives and non-relatives over the years. He has also employed countless individuals over the years, most of whom have benefited significantly from their work relationship with Ellis, including his strong work ethic and the focus on the customer.

I can honestly say that I've known Ellis Crook for my entire life. I was probably first introduced to him at some type of family gathering, because Ellis is my uncle – the youngest brother of my mother, Edith Crook Sewell. (Yes, my mother was a Crook!) Even though we're related, I believe I've seen him from the same perspective as others who have known him well. I've even had difficulty, like some of you, in comprehending what Uncle Ellis is saying. His speech is sometimes faster than my brain wants to process, but he usually gets his point across. Bottom-line, he's an amazing individual who has truly had his ups and downs; still, he has persevered while helping others and giving back to make a positive difference.

Ellis' father, Arry Lee Crook, sold Ellis the family business, Crook's Food Mart, in 1960. It was a small grocery store with narrow aisles where the Hit 'N Run convenience store is now located. After operating the Food Mart and working many hours every day, Ellis wanted to fulfill his vision of having a larger, more modern grocery store for the people in the Senoia area. This vision became a reality when what is now Crook's Marketplace was opened in 1981. What many people don't realize is the huge gamble that Ellis took in pursuing this dream. Senoia was not thriving in 1981 like it has been more recently. People were moving away and working elsewhere. The downtown area had been "drying up" for quite some time. I remember talking in the 1970s with my father, Ray Sewell, about taking over his General Merchandise store. He showed me his books and discouraged me from following in his footsteps.

As Ellis' daughter, Cheryl Crook Thompson, pointed out in a Facebook post in February of 2020, her mother (Ellis' wife, Pat Yarbrough Crook) also believed in Ellis' dream enough that "she gave him all HER money to invest in this venture, and she agreed to let him mortgage EVERYTHING they owned for the financing. Might not have seemed like a lot of money to some folks but it was all they had."

Cousin Cheryl also stated that "for several years afterward, my dad was sweating making the payments. He developed heart trouble, ended up with a quadruple bypass, but he only took three days away from the store."

And at age 88+ as his book, *Senoia Boy*, is about to be published, Ellis Crook is still working practically every day at Crook's Marketplace or transporting items between the Marketplace in Senoia and the Food Outlet store that he and his son, Greg, operate in Newnan, or driving to the Farmers' Market in Forest Park, and on and on and on.

He is a rare entity in that he was born and raised in the same town (Senoia) that he has continued to serve throughout his adulthood as a businessman and as a civic-minded individual. He has continued to worship in the same church that his parents took him to as a young boy. On a personal note, when my wife Vicki and I were first married and had moved into our home on Clearwater Lake in the Sharpsburg area, it was Ellis Crook who invited us to become active in the church. It had been my church, too, as I grew up, but we hadn't started regularly attending yet when we first moved back to the area. Through Ellis' encouragement, we did–and we still do. Ellis has been a positive influence on so many of us, and he has given back to organizations and to individuals in ways we will never fully know.

Because of his commitments and his good acts, he has been recognized over the years. A few of the examples of such recognition would include being presented with Senoia's Legacy award in 2012, receiving a Quilt of Valor in 2017 for his military service, and receiving the "Scout of the Year" award at the Senoia United Methodist Church for his "dedication, passion, and support of the Scouts."

Uncle Ellis was included along with Paul McKnight, Jr., Jimmy Hutchinson, and Frank (Buddy) Hollberg III in a special picture by Fine Arts photographer Gary Gruby, titled "Four Gentlemen of Senoia" that hangs in the museum operated by the Senoia Area Historical Society (SAHS).

Still, he will never be "paid back" sufficiently for his contributions (many of which we will never know about) nor does he expect to be.

Ellis Crook has had a genuine relationship with customers, family, and friends for his entire life. He doesn't sugar-coat things. He doesn't promise more than he can deliver. He will, however, tell you the genuine truth and work with you the best he can.

Ellis is proud of the fact that–as an older adult–he lives within sight of where he lived with his family as a young boy. I'm proud that he has made the commitment to live his life in Senoia, operate his businesses in Senoia, and serve the people of Senoia and beyond. I'm proud, too, that he has served this wonderful community so faithfully as an adult. As a Board member of the Senoia Area Historical Society which works diligently to help preserve and promote the history of the Senoia area, I am humbled by the history that "Uncle Ellis" has made throughout his lifetime, and the memories that he has captured in his book, Senoia Boy. The SAHS truly appreciates his donation of the Senoia Boy manuscript to our organization, and we are excited about sharing it with those who want to read his memoirs and better understand what his life and Senoia were like "back in the day."

Hal Sewell, nephew and
Senoia Area Historical Society Board Member, 2020

Hal Sewell and Ellis Crook
Photo courtesy of Senoia Area Historical Society

Ellis Crook in 2019 Memorial Day parade
Photo courtesy of Hal Sewell

Why I wrote this book

Many years ago now, the Senoia Area Historical Society held one of its popular progressive dinners, where homeowners in the historic district host a course for the evening's meal, and diners move from house to house while eating salads, the main course, desserts, and so on, while getting to see the inside of these (sometimes newly renovated) homes.

One year, I attended the progressive dinner and ended up seated in a small den behind the kitchen during the dessert course. My daughter had been looking for me and discovered about twenty folks gathered round while I told tales about my younger days and how Senoia used to be.

Senoia has seen a lot of new people move into town in recent years, and I have been amazed to learn that even they like hearing about Senoia's history, sometimes more than the people who have lived here all their lives. I've also looked around and realized that I'm one of the few still living who experienced or heard these stories firsthand.

With this memoir, I have not intended to write a history of the town or even a chronological account of my life. Instead, just sit down in that den with me as I tell you some stories.

I hope you'll appreciate hearing them as told by this "Senoia boy."

"Senoia" can be pronounced three different ways:

Tourists: Si-Noi-Uh
Transplants: Si-Noh-Uh
Locals: Si-Noy (Rhymes with "boy")
Any way you say it, it's home to me.

All that is written in this book is solely my own recollection to the best of my ability. Most everyone alive at the time of many of these events is no longer here, so there's not many to dispute me.

About the cover art

I gave each of my children this picture of me at about five years of age, standing in a cotton field with a cotton sack and a straw hat. I told them I'd better see that picture hanging in a prominent place whenever I visited so they would never forget where they came from (and might have to go back to if they didn't work hard).

Ellis Crook, around 5 years old, picking cotton
Photo courtesy of the Crook family

Ellis Crook with his parents
Photo courtesy of Hal Sewell

A heritage born in Senoia

My father, Arry Lee (A. L.) Crook, was born on February 19, 1888, in the area of Bethel Church on Luther Bailey Road in Senoia. My mother, Leola Mae Addy, was also born and raised in Senoia. Her people migrated from Newberry, South Carolina, with many other families in the early 1800s.

Dad went to college in Carrollton at the A&M School, the forerunner of West Georgia College, and was dismissed after being caught in the apple orchard with a lady friend. He came home, and in his early twenties, he opened a store in Senoia.

Two memorable stories were told to me by my dad, Arry Lee Crook.

One time, he was dating a girl at a community about four miles above Fayetteville. On the way back home around midnight, with his horse steadily pulling the buggy up Porter Hill between Bernard Road and Starr's Mill, he saw a headless ghost coming at him, so he pulled his pistol out of its hiding place and laid it on the seat of the buggy. Just as he got about even with the ghost, he was relieved to discover that it was only a large black woman dressed in white and a smaller (nearly invisible, in the dark) black man dressed in black.

Around 1910, about three miles below Senoia and along the railroad was the Chestlehurst community (near where the Brooks community is now). There was a brickyard there that employed all black men digging the mud from the pits to make brick. The bricks were then put on the railway that ran to Griffin.

Dad was leaving the brickyard at Chestlehurst one night in his buggy, and they had apprehended a black man wanted for murder who was working there, so they tied him up and put him on the back of Dad's buggy to take him to Senoia and put him on a train to send him to Atlanta. While the buggy was bouncing its way along Chestlehurst Road to Senoia, the prisoner broke loose from his ties. Dad saw what was happening, so he got his gun, threw out all the cartridges, then threw the gun out across the woods. When he looked back, he saw the prisoner heading for the woods, no doubt to find the gun. But Dad had popped the horse, and he was up the road toward Senoia at a galloping speed, for he had a fast-trotting, beautiful mare and a good buggy.

My dad is written up in Carolyn Cary's history of Fayette County because the owner of the first store in the Chestlehurst community built a second store across the railroad track and sold my dad the first building—a small, long building shaped like a shotgun house.

The other store owner laid a shotgun across his lap and

dared anyone to trade with my dad. Dad was quoted as stating that he also had a shotgun.

The brickyard later was closed, and everybody moved out. Meanwhile, the person operating the store for Dad in Senoia had extended too much credit and couldn't collect the money that was owed, so Dad went out of business completely.

Somewhere along the way, he turned to hauling freight from the depot, using mules and dray to carry it to the stores uptown. After being a merchant, he no doubt found this degrading, but he had to make a living. He and my mother had to move seven times in seven years because either they could not pay the rent or the owner sold the house they lived in and they had to move.

In later years, Dad bought land and a nice home where the blue hangar is located at Tinsley Way and Highway 16 in Senoia. He also built a big livestock barn, constructed mostly using money borrowed from Farmers and Merchants Bank.

Dad had harvested a big crop of cotton, approximately fifty bales weighing around four hundred pounds each, and the price of cotton was climbing and had already reached forty-four cents per pound. My grandfather told Dad to hold on to it because the cotton would reach fifty cents a pound, but it did not. The price started dropping. My dad finally sold out at thirteen cents a pound, and Farmers and Merchants Bank foreclosed on him, and my dad lost his house. My parents and my older siblings had to move to the old Candy Bridges house at 96 Luther Bailey Road, where we rented from Mrs. Mattie Thurmond. We farmed the land and finally bought the place a few years later for $1,800. I grew up in this two-story barn of a house, located just beyond the Bank of Coweta. This house appears on the 1898 map of Senoia, and the daughter and grandson of Chief William McIntosh, who signed the Treaty of Indian Springs in 1825, are buried on the property that belonged to the Bridges family.

I remember that house was really cold in the winter. There was a wood stove in the kitchen and a fireplace in the living room (which we never used unless company came), and my parents had a Warm Morning model wood and coal heater. That's where we sat most evenings in the winter, listening to the radio. I had no heat in my bedroom and, because I was the baby of the family, slept with my parents many nights. The water bucket in the kitchen would freeze in the winter, and we had to chop through the ice every morning. I vowed I would never live in an older house because of the lack of central heating, and you always have to spend money on these houses.

We had to draw water from the well for drinking, cooking, bathing, and watering the animals (horses, pigs, mules, and chickens). Our outhouse was located beyond the hedgerow, and it was fancy in that it had TWO seats, with an old Sears and Roebuck catalog to use for toilet paper. There's a story about chickens and poop, but I won't go into it here.

I was the youngest child by eight years, and my mother was forty-four years old when I was born. My oldest brother, Julian, graduated high school the same week of my birth, so you can figure there were many years between the first and last babies in our family. Since most of my siblings were leaving home or gone, I had to learn to do a lot of chores my parents had previously counted on them to do. My early childhood consisted of feeding the chickens, slopping the hogs, drawing water from the well, gathering up the eggs, and working in the garden—all with encouragement from a peach tree switch. (Note to younger readers, switches were small branches from trees used as corporal punishment, usually administered across the legs or butt.)

At age nine, I was taught how to milk cows by a black man named Preacher Murry. He outsmarted me somehow, and I became the cow milker, as Dad did not have to pay me. I milked the cows early in the morning before school on school days and just before dark every day, including Sunday. I graduated from high school and milking at the same time, as I refused to do this anymore and we could obtain milk from the store.

I was picking cotton by age five, and my record, at approximately age eleven, was 125 pounds in one evening. But I was tending three rows between my dad and the high school principal and was forced to keep up with them. The principal was Sam C. Mashburn. He walked with a limp, but he picked cotton with us because we needed the help, and he needed the money. Principals and schoolteachers had to supplement their incomes in those days even more than they do now.

When I was nine years old, I learned how to plant cotton by guiding a mule pulling the cotton planter. This was a slightly easier job for me, if not for the mule.

My mother worked hard, and while she never weighed more than one hundred pounds, she never shied from physical work. She hoed in the garden continuously during the summer to get rid of weeds. She cooked three meals a day (sometimes for just us, but often in the summer for the hands that worked in the fields, too) and also gathered, cleaned, cooked, and canned enough food to get us through the winter. I occasionally helped her in the kitchen, too, especially when she would make her homemade noodles. We would pick peaches and apples and dry them on the roof and make fried pies with the dried fruit. Mr. Jim Baggarly Sr. loved those pies so much, he was always first in line at any dinner at the Senoia United Methodist Church to get one or two for dessert before they ran out. My mother was always working. I remember even at night she would crochet and darn and sew until her head nodded and she dropped the needle in her lap. Then she'd jerk awake and start her needlework again until the house grew cold and it was time to go to bed.

Hog-killing time

After the first frost but before it got really cold—around 29 to 32 degrees Fahrenheit—it was hog-killing time. We killed and processed the hog completely, from curing the hams and middlings to making sausage, liver pudding, and souse meat and cooking the fatback into lard.

I was taught to shoot the hog in the sinkhole of the forehead (between the eyes), then cut its throat to let it bleed out while it hung on a tripod of poles. It took a good sharp knife to cut through the skin of the stomach, but you had to be careful to cut only so deep in order that the intestines were not cut. Then a circular cut was made around the tail of the hog so the intestines, liver, and other parts could be separated from the backbone.

After gutting the hog, we placed it in a barrel full of hot water. At times, we built a fire at the rear of the barrel to heat the water. We used lime on the skin to help make the hog's hair come off easier as we scraped the skin with a knife.

The black helpers were given the skin after we cut the fatback to make lard. They chopped and cooked the skins in ovens and had pork skins to eat before store-bought pork skins were ever available. Souse meat was made from the head, and the liver was made into liver pudding. We cut the meat out of the backbone, fried it, and called it tenderloin. It was the same thing as the center of a pork chop you buy today.

We gave the intestines we did not need to the black help, and they made what we called chitterlings (or "chitlins"), which were chopped and eaten boiled or, after boiling, battered and fried. After slinging out the insides of the intestines to empty them, you turned them inside out and scraped them on a board to clean them. You'd have to wash them several times before they were ready to cook.

We salted down the hams and bellies with a fine salt to cure the meat so that it didn't have to be refrigerated. The temperature couldn't be too far below freezing because salt needed to soak into the meat to cure it. Some people would take the hams up in a few weeks, soak them with sorghum syrup (to keep the flies off), and wrap them with brown paper before leaving them hanging in the smokehouse to finish drying. We made sausage from the trimmings off the streak o' lean and front shoulders of the hog. Tenderloin was always one of my favorites. We made it by cutting out the filet in the pork loin then cubing it by using a hammer with sharp teeth, much like a meat tenderizer, and battering each piece with egg and flour before frying it. After the filet was cut, the meat between the bones was cut in pieces, boiled, and eaten with (mostly root) vegetables or peas or beans that had been dried and stored for winter. Any meat that fell off the bone was placed in quart jars and sealed for later use.

My mother made "press meat," or souse, from the hog's head, which I love. She also made liver pudding, which I detest to this day. The sausage meat was stuffed into the smaller intestines of the hog, which had been cleaned by scraping them and running hot water through them. When the sausage was stuffed and came out of the sausage mill snout to fill up the intestines, I had to take a needle and punch holes in the intestines, as they sometimes bloated with air. Then we hung the sausages on rafters in the smokehouse, where green hickory wood was put in a pot to burn slowly and smoke along with red hot peppers to keep the flies away. This slow fire would dry the sausage so it would be preserved and not rot.

In the summertime, we stored Irish potatoes (small, round potatoes that grew under vines) in the loft of the smokehouse. We also placed onions in old stockings with a twist between each onion to separate them and let them air dry as they hung in the smokehouse.

My experience in killing and processing a hog really paid off later, as I made sausage in the meat market of the grocery store we ran from 1947 until I built the supermarket in 1981.

Crook siblings, Hugh, Ellis, Edith, Alva, and Julian
Photo courtesy of Hal Sewell

Brantley Institute
Photo courtesy of Senoia Area Historical Society

Starting school

I walked to school at Brantley Institute in Senoia (also called Senoia High School) until 1946, when it was closed. My dad drove me to school only if it was raining or extremely cold. I had four much older siblings—Julian, Edith, Alva, and Hugh. My brother Hugh, being eight years older than I, had graduated from Brantley Institute in the spring of 1937, and so I started that first fall with no brothers or sister at that school to tattle on me.

We had built forts on the old school ground in Senoia, and since there were big oak trees on the school property, we got into acorn-throwing battles with each other. It's a wonder we did not put out someone's eye.

It was a tough twelve years from the time I was born, as my dad worked in the fields and was down on his luck. He knew his ability to succeed was great, but he couldn't borrow any money. One Christmas, I received a pair of overalls and a few apples and oranges as my gift, as he told me he could not even borrow a quarter. This sad tale is one my children repeated back to me so often, it has lost its effect. No doubt this made me want to have a better life for my family and myself, as I have nearly always worked twelve-hour or longer days.

We weren't the only ones scrambling to make a living however we could. Even up until the 1970s, Clifford Amey was supplementing her income by making a special "home brew" from raisins and Blue Ribbon malt. No doubt this was a popular drink among some citizens, as one Christmas Eve, my daughter and I stopped by about 9 p.m. to deliver a fruit basket and some food. I went up to the porch, knocked on the door, and yelled in a deep voice, "Ho, ho, ho, Clifford!" She asked, "Who is it?" I said, "It's SANTA CLAUS, Clifford! Come to the door!" Clifford thought it was one of her customers coming by for a little taste of home brew before going home, and she yelled, "Get off my porch, N-----!" I tried again. "Clifford, it's Santa Claus!" but then I remembered she had a shotgun, and I decided it would be best to leave the basket and skedaddle on out of there. (I did call her later and tell her to go check her porch so she'd find the food before someone else did.)

Peach orchards of
the thirties and forties

During the 1930s and 1940s, we had peach orchards on the north side of Senoia as well as on Highway 16 East and where McKnight Road is now. These orchards, and a packing shed that sat alongside the railroad track across from the downtown Senoia park on Seavy Street, were owned by Frank P. Daniel Sr. and Oscar Mann. Other large orchards were located on Rock House Road and were owned by Carl McKnight and Bill Rowe. Their packing shed is now a horse barn across from Butcher's Dairy, where Senoia's first building, an old green house made out of rock, once stood and for which the road was named.

My father and Mr. Emmett Freeman, the hermit brother of Bob Walt Freeman, worked at the McKnight orchards, and their job was to keep tabs on how many buckets of peaches each picker picked and pay accordingly. It was said that Mr. Emmett could stand in the middle of the orchard and keep the neatest record while holding a little (free) snuff booklet in his hand, writing his figures in this little booklet with the likeness of a can of dental snuff on the outside and blank pages on the inside.

At Daniel and Mann orchards, I worked for Richard Orr, a son-in-law of the Mangets of Newnan and owners of the orchards. I graded peaches and made rings of top-grade peaches to place on top of the other peaches before putting a lid on the basket so they'd look nice when the boxes were opened. Box cars sat on the track next to the packing shed and had ice placed in them prior to loading and departure for the northern markets. Today, the only orchards nearby— the ones as of this writing—are the Carroll Farms orchards in Woodbury and Gregg's in Hollonville. Now all peaches are shipped by truck, which transports them much faster, and the peaches are easier to refrigerate.

In the spring of 1942, my father rented a young peach orchard from Miss Margaret McKnight, the spinster sister of Paul McKnight Sr. The orchard was located one mile east of Georgia Highway 85 on Georgia Highway 16. Dad agreed to pay her a stipend for each bushel of peaches picked. He did real well on this venture, as he had worked hard in the orchards, pruning and spraying, so he knew how to manage the orchard.

We set the peaches out by the road and sold them for fifty cents per bushel to Pomona Products Canning Company in Griffin, Georgia, and they were canned under the Sunshine label. He did so well that she would not rent the orchard to him again. This was the first time he had gotten out of debt since 1931 (the year I was born and the beginning of the

Great Depression).

My father made enough from the peach sales to pay off my mother's brothers and sister for the money he had borrowed from my grandfather John Addy prior to his death approximately eight years earlier.

In February of 1943, at the height of World War II, Dad opened a store in a building he rented from Mr. Walt Hubbard.

Mr. Hubbard had been operating the little wooden service station where Synovus Bank (formerly the Bank of Coweta) is now located on Highway 16. Mr. Walt had worked for the railroad and had made more money there, no doubt, than he was making at the store.

The building belonged to his brother, Mr. Lewis Hubbard. Dad sold two mules and raised five hundred dollars. We paid rent of one cent a gallon for the gas sold and used the five hundred dollars to buy inventory. World War II was underway, and you could sell rationed meat or gas, along with other foodstuffs, and make a good living. In those days, we had a cold-water drink or soda box and a six-hole ice cream box, a pair of baby scales to weigh things on, and we made change out of an empty cigar box.

Since meat was rationed, it was often hard to come by. We could get streak o' lean meat at the store more often, and we would cut it in small pieces and hide it under the counter or put it up in small packages for our regular customers. When the local housewives saw that meat truck come around during the day, they would try to buy up the streak o' lean, but we saved it for our regular customers who were out working during the day.

Back when gasoline was rationed, the regular price was ninety cents for five gallons of gas, but you also had to have a ration coupon in order to buy it. The bootlegged price was fifty cents per gallon, a 270 percent markup. If you didn't have a ration coupon but couldn't pay the bootlegged price, you had to know someone who knew someone at the Office of Price Administration (OPA) board or ration board.

During World War II, Dad bought a pickup truck simply for the tires, as no tires could be obtained, and put them on his car. If he needed to haul something with the truck, he would jack up the car and switch the tires to the truck.

The Coca-Cola Company correctly predicted that we were going to be drawn into World War II, and based on that prediction, they knew sugar would be rationed. So they sent my Uncle Dorris Austin, who was married to my mother's sister Alice, to Baltimore, Maryland, with the instructions to rent all the warehouses he could and buy and store all the sugar he could so they could keep producing Coca-Cola, as there was no substitute for sugar at that time. Not only was sugar rationed, but also the boats bringing sugar from Cuba were under threat of being torpedoed.

Bootlegging was not just confined to gas and sugar. The

bread delivery person brought bread out of Atlanta each day, but he made more money hauling bootlegged meat, frozen whiting fish, and any other hard-to-get items than he ever did on the sale of bread. This was of no knowledge to the bread company owners. We would get in five to six ten-pound boxes of frozen whiting fish on Saturday morning and had to sell it that day because we had no place to store frozen products.

When Dad was operating in that building, he had a black man who had farmed with us and then also worked at the store, doing tasks such as pumping gas and cleaning. When the man died, his wife went to draw her Social Security check. We had never paid into the government any deductions on our part or his part, therefore after a lot of letter writing and threats about the matter, we finally settled that for a sum of money.

Dad never kept any books on the profitability of the business, as his barometer of success was how much money was in the bank. If I had not kept books of a fashion on the store and if Ray Sewell had not filed the estimated income tax, Dad would have probably wound up in jail for tax evasion. It's legal to avoid but illegal to evade, and Dad believed in avoiding this manner of taxation.

When we were in business in that old wooden building, we sold gasoline to a local gin for their trucks that hauled cotton, and Dad gave them a discount on gas due to the amount they purchased. He always sent me to collect the money at the gin owner's office. The owner would keep me sitting for an hour or more, as he didn't like for the money to leave his account, so that was why Dad sent me to collect it.

The gin owner had peach pickers who worked in the peach orchard, and they were paid according to how many bushels of peaches they'd picked. That owner would wait until Saturday night about 10 p.m. to pay them, when all the other stores were closed. In the meantime, the pickers sat around on the outjuttings of the building, and by the time they got paid, all the other stores were closed, so they had to make their purchases for the week at the owner's "company store," which was conveniently still open.

The wholesale grocery houses of the 1940s were located in Griffin: Griffin Grocery Company, H. V. Kell Company, City Wholesale, and Service Wholesale, all of which met their demise due to competition and changing times. Very few companies or people last in the grocery business the length of time that we have on the corners of Highway 16 and Broad Street. The following persons or stores were selling groceries during the period from 1946 until their closure: C. P. Daniel & Son, P. R. McKnight Sr., Addy's Grocery (Eulys, Kate, Isadore), Crook & Sewell (Hugh Crook and Ray Sewell), Cook's Market (Howell and Evelyn Cook), Hollberg's, and in the same location, B. A. Nolan's Grocery and later Bruce Fry Grocery, which was located at the bottom of the hill where the Senoia Coffee & Café is today. Mr. B. A. Nolan operated his grocery store in the front building (which still stands), and in the back of the building, which has since been torn away, he published Senoia's first regular newspaper, the *Enterprise Gazette*. Sometimes on Saturdays, my dad worked at Nolan's Grocery. Dad would occasionally bring home red link sausages, which were a treat for us (and still are for me).

Cigarettes sold for one cent each, and anybody could buy them, no matter their age. In those days, the brands were mostly Camels, Lucky Strikes, and Old Gold.

Sugar was scarce, and if it was bought on the black market, the bootleggers making whiskey on the branch would buy—and did buy—all they could get plus gray shorts (wheat bran) to use at their stills in making moonshine. There were lucrative moonshine operations in the area—Haralson, on Line Creek at Digby and also Padgett Road in Fayette County, near where the clay pits were dug. Finally, after Prohibition, store-bought whiskey was cheaper than bootlegged whiskey, and the bootleggers started going out of business.

After we'd been in the building four years, Lewis Hubbard, Walt Hubbard's brother and the owner of the building, wanted my daddy to move out. Eugene Talmadge was either running for or serving as governor, and Lewis Hubbard made his presence known as a Talmadge supporter at the Capitol and elsewhere and got a state job. O. S. Miller, who clerked at McKnight's General Store, had also gotten to be a backslapping buddy of Eugene Talmadge, and he chimed in to get on the good side of Lewis Hubbard and did a good job of what we call brownnosing with Hubbard. We found out that Mr. Miller had rented the building out from under us for one and one half cents a gallon on gas. My father said he would pay that much extra rent, but Lewis Hubbard wanted my dad out of the building. Mr. Hubbard came over and was going to physically move him out, but Dad used some choice words to let Lewis Hubbard know that he needed to suppress his demands for us to leave until we got a new building constructed, and that's exactly what happened.

O. S. Miller did not last in the business very long. Later, Newnan Oil Company bought the property after the demise of Miller's business.

Ellis at Crook's Food Mart
Photo courtesy of Senoia Area Historical Society

The family store opens
for business in 1947

Dad got J. B. Hutchinson to sell him a 100-by-100-foot lot on the corner of Highway 16 and Broad Street for four hundred dollars and a handshake contract saying that we would sell Hutchinson's distributorship gasoline, a contract we honored for many years until they quit the dealership. This 30-by-40-foot building was one of the first cement block buildings in Senoia after World War II. In 1947, we moved into this building with two gas pumps and two 500-gallon underground tanks. This is where Crook's Hit-N-Run is now (but not the same building).

While we were operating in this building, we took orders over the phone from the in-town people, then we delivered their groceries and charged them. On Friday nights and Saturdays, the black families walked into town to buy groceries, and we would haul them and their groceries, including, at times, kerosene back to their homes. Because the kerosene could splash from the can and ruin the groceries, we always put a small potato piece as a stopper in the spout of the can.

Brantley Institute, also known as Senoia High School, was consolidated with Starr High School in 1946, and the consolidation was named East Coweta High School. Mrs. Lee Hand, who had been at the high school since the early 1920s and taught all my brothers and sister and me, finished her career by offering private Latin lessons taught around her dining room table during the 1946-1947 school year. She was paid by the county, as they did not offer Latin in the newly merged high school. The students in Senoia who had one year of Latin before the merger needed the second year for it to count toward their graduation.

I graduated from high school at the same time I turned seventeen, in 1948, because back in those days in Georgia, secondary schooling ended after eleventh grade. My dad said that if I wanted to work in the store, he would pay me thirty-five dollars a week and board. He bought me a car from a former mule trader who was in the auto business. It was a gray Oldsmobile Torpedo, and I made twenty-dollar-a-week payments on it, so I had to hustle for other means to pick up enough money to keep my numerous dating engagements. When I was nineteen, my father contracted tuberculosis and was confined to bed rest for two years, so I had to operate the store. I took the money home each night in a cigar box for Dad to count.

My future brother-in-law, Ray S. Sewell, came to Senoia in the mid-1930s to keep books for C. P. Daniel & Son. The owner at that time was Frank Daniel Sr., the son of Charles Perdue Daniel. The founder's mother was a Purdue and a relative of Ray Sewell's parents. They had two great souls working there, including William (Bill) Addy, my mother's first cousin, who was around fifty, and Mr. Oscar Brown, the grandfather of Catherine Ann Brown Barnette. Mr. Brown also was the justice of the peace for this area at that time.

Ellis with classmates at Brantley Institute
Photo courtesy of the Crook family

Senoia United Methodist Church, Photo courtesy of Senoia UMC

The JOY class at Senoia United Methodist Church
Photo courtesy of the estate of Melvin Cheek

Faith, family, and the farm

Senoia United Methodist Church has a long history of people attending in their youth and later. My sister, Edith, and brothers Alva and Hugh were driven to Sunday school in a buggy by our oldest brother, Julian L. Crook. Julian said he tied the mule to the big oak tree that used to sit in the middle of what is now the church parking lot. The tree was taken down a few years ago to make the church parking lot larger. At this time, we lived at the house at the corner of Tinsley Way and Highway 16, so it was about a mile to the church each way.

We also farmed a tract of land at 8334 Highway 16 (where my house sits now) as well as forty-nine acres behind this tract on Crook Road that were bought from Miss Margaret McKnight, the aunt of P. R. McKnight Jr. At age eleven, I planted cotton with a mule-drawn planter that kicked the seed out as a spoke wheel turned in the hopper on the thirty-four-acre tract. When you took the cotton to the gin house to be ginned, you swapped your cottonseed that came out of the cotton for ground cottonseed meal and hulls of the cottonseed that were used in feeding the milk cows on the farm, and this made them give more milk.

When kids from in town would visit and I was milking, I got a kick out of holding the cow's tit, squeezing the devil out of it, and aiming at the mouth of one of these kids while they sat on the plank wall and watched me milk. Sometimes the cow would quickly put her foot into the bucket, letting some manure fall inside. We just took the milk on to the house, and we always strained the milk through a cloth. Nobody had the Department of Agriculture inspector back then.

I began milking a cow at age nine and milked at least one every morning and every night. A lesson I learned in hand milking a cow is that it's not wise to sit the milk bucket on the ground and then just begin squeezing and pulling. Not only do you have to aim well, if you put the bucket closer (like on a box), the cow can kick the bucket and knock it away from you while you're milking. I learned to secure the bucket in between my legs while milking the cow.

If you have a large enough hand, you can place the third finger between two tits on the right and two tits on the left and milk all four tits at once.

We fed the cows cottonseed hulls and cottonseed meal produced from the cottonseed we got when we had the cotton ginned. We added a few pinches of soda, and we kept a salt block in the pasture so the cows would lick it and drink more water and give more milk.

I was playing cowboy with two milk cows one time and

tied the horns of each cow together, and did I make a mistake. The cows started running across the pasture, and just as they got to a big pine tree, one cow jerked the other cow into the tree and broke off one of its horns.

That ruined the sale of a good milk cow. I forget whether Daddy tore my britches up or not, but Daddy tried to have an extra cow or bull to sell in case of a money emergency.

We had very little money to spend, but most people in the 1930s were scarce on money.

I peddled buttermilk for five cents a quart. Money from this and milk and butter paid for my piano lessons from Miss Belle Jones at Senoia School for four years. Miss Jones was the great-grandmother of Randy, Bill, and Brantly Todd through the lineage of their mother, Mary Brantly Tribble Todd. Her middle name, Brantly, was no doubt from Dr. F. M. Brantly, for whom the Brantley Institute on Clark Street was named. (It's not clear why the school's name was spelled with an "e" while the doctor—even on his tombstone in the City Cemetery—and descendants named after him were known as Brantly.) This school had a red clay outdoor basketball court and a baseball field. These were the only facilities for recreation. We had no air-conditioning in the auditorium, which was a fairly decent size for that era. When the afternoon sun was boiling down, it made for a sleepy, dull geography lesson. During later years, this building was still in use, and a drive to build a gymnasium was started. Dr. Fischer of

Fischer Road in Sharpsburg was contacted, and being a foremost doctor in Atlanta, he donated quite a sum of money to build this gym with a kitchen and offices up front. This gym was used until the school closed down.

Some forward-thinking citizens knew we needed jobs for people living here, so we had a man by the name of Shapiro put in a cutting-and-sewing operation in the building. He didn't last too long, though, and then the Carter Company, maker of baby clothes, was contacted by someone in Senoia to possibly lease the building. Plans began for the Carter Company to start a small plant in the gym building and train people, then they would build a large plant here in Senoia. Well, one of the descendants of a donor who had given a grand total of $12.50 (one-sixteenth of the original $200 purchase price) to help purchase the land on which the school and gym were located knew there was a clause in the deed saying that if the property ever ceased to be used for school purposes, it would revert to the donors of the property. A big uproar ensued between two men at a Lions Club meeting in the veterans building in the Senoia park. The wife of one of those men actually called Needham, Massachusetts, to berate the Carter Company about taking the gym away from the children of the town. (Her forefather was one of the $12.50 donors.)

The Carter Company immediately ceased plans to come to Senoia. Not long after that, the building was ablaze one night, and since all the floors had been treated with oil over the years, the building burned fast. Most people presumed that a teenaged descendant of the original donors was involved in the loss of this historical school building.

In the 1970s, the front offices of the gym briefly served as an office for Senoia's first full-time doctor in many years, Dr. Marcos Dones, until he could relocate. Later, when the inside or gym part of the building had fallen into disrepair, the City of Senoia used it for storage and repair of equipment. In 2008, the city had the old tin building with its brick facade torn down and removed from the property. The land was later divided into lots for sale by the city, and a number of homes have since been built on these lots. This property is on Clark Street, next to the closed-down Norfolk Southern (formerly Central of Georgia) railroad tracks.

*Before and after views of the most recent renovations to
downtown Senoia's Main Street
Photo courtesy of Stephen Sweet*

Senoia in the time of train travel

The Atlantic Coast Line Railroad located on Seavy Street had a depot, and I remember seeing the telegraph key in front of the window facing the tracks. Melvin Cheek trained to learn Morse code and operate the key. Mr. Phil Phillips and his wife, Miss Mary Phillips, were the main operators of the key and the depot. Miss Mary was much younger than her husband and quite an attractive lady with many admirers.

Mr. or Mrs. Phillips would clamp messages to a big round loop at the end of a rod. As the train came through, someone on the train would extend their arm and catch the loop with the messages attached as the train moved through town. During the late 1930s and early 1940s, we had a so-called streamline train, and each passenger car had the name of a Florida destination, such as Flagler Beach, Palm Beach, and so on for each passenger car being pulled down the Atlantic Coast Line Railroad.

Back in the days of steam engines, a pumping station was located on the branch that runs from Marimac Lakes, and it was located on the south side of the railroad track. Water was pumped back up the track to the depot on Seavy Street for the steam engines. Sleeping in a house close to the track when the trains blew their whistle as they went by, you kind of got accustomed to the noise.

Ellis Crook during military service
Photo courtesy of the Crook family

My dad as a businessman

I was in line at the funeral home visitation for Paul McKnight Jr., who had died a few days before on March 22, 2009. I had a conversation with Wilbur Nixon, son of Gordon Nixon, who grew up on Old Highway 85 and Dolly Nixon Road, and he recalled the time that he was working for Stacy Whatley and remodeling houses in Griffin. It was a dirty job, and he didn't like it. So Mr. Whatley told Wilbur to report Monday morning to work for A. L. Crook, as his son was in the service, and he needed help in the store since Mr. Crook was recovering from tuberculosis and couldn't come to work every day. Wilbur and I discussed the fact that Dad sold overalls, khaki pants, shirts, and brogan shoes. One Sunday morning, someone needed a belt, and Dad sold them the belt out of his pants. (It was a good thing he did not have a cough—meaning he would have been contagious—at that time.)

Dad also bought old Stetson hats that had been cleaned and re-blocked and sold them for five dollars each. Wilbur said he enjoyed working with my dad. Later, Wilbur obtained a good job in the transportation department of Ford in Hapeville, shipping new autos, before he retired and the plant closed.

Dad never accumulated a great amount of money, as he was constantly improving the business. He added onto the original cinder block building three times before I bought the business in 1960. While I was in the Army, someone broke into the store and stole what they believed to be a safe, but it was actually a heavy metal fold-down-and-lock cabinet that had metal folding leaves inside, with metal clips on each leaf to hold each customer's charges.

The next morning, there were no longer any records of the amount each customer owed, as their tickets were in the stolen metal cabinet. Dad had to take their word for how much they had charged and owed. In about a week, someone found the cabinet in a field, and my dad got it back. It was amazing how some folks had lied about the amount they owed, thinking Dad would have to take their word for it and take a lesser amount.

Sometime between 1943 and 1947, Dad sold sugar and gray wheat shorts to Louie Flournoy, who used it to make liquor. Dad let him charge his groceries and no doubt other products, and Louie got caught bootlegging moonshine and was jailed. While serving time, he sent word to Dad by his wife about where the liquor was buried out in the field around his house. Dad sent John Alvin Watson, a longtime black employee, to get the alcoholic spirits. John Alvin and his wife sold it—by the glass—across the street. John Alvin made some money to live on and paid Dad the money the moonshiner owed him. It was just old-fashioned bartering. John Alvin's house was across the road from where the big oak tree stands on the west side of Luther Bailey Road on Highway 16.

John Alvin had several brothers. One was Mack Watson, who delivered for Hollberg's Pharmacy and Grocery. On some trips, he made more money by selling moonshine from under the seat of the truck than Hollberg's did from their own sale. Another brother, Joe Watson, was working for Dad when I got out of the Army, and another, Rufus Watson, after his retirement from Clayton County, drove my truck to Atlanta and hauled produce and other goods for me. Their brother Olin Watson was married to Tommie Lee "Sis" Watson, who was the nanny who helped raise my children— Cheryl, Ken, and Greg—while my wife worked. Once all the children were in school, Sis moved on to a custodial job at the local Farmers and Merchants Bank.

Sis copied recipes from my wife, Pat (who had originally taught home economics and had a trove of recipes), and became well known for her cake baking. Pat financed a house on Couch Street so Olin and Sis could buy it. She also financed one across the road for Lizzie Mae Rush, the mother of Margaret Rush Amey. Both paid for their houses at a very low interest rate, and I transferred the deeds paid in full. Lizzie Mae Rush was the housekeeper for Parker and

Frances Cleveland, and sometime after her death, Margaret's husband, George Amey, became their reliable worker and a friend of the family.

After the original baseball stadium opened in Atlanta near the Capitol, I sent John Alvin Watson with Greg, Ken, and Jim Hutchinson to a game at the stadium. That was a big time back then, but on the way home, the muffler fell off the car. Not only did they have a roaring good time at the ball game, but they also "roared" all the way back to Senoia.

Civil War tales in my family

During the Civil War, salt was not available to all people, and they would go to the smokehouse where meat had been processed and dig up and then boil the dirt, somehow deriving salt from this procedure. If they thought any soldiers were coming through, they hid the animals in the woods, as the army would take them for food.

My mother told me that her ancestors had a fiddle, and knowing that any Yankees who came through would take anything from the house, her family wrapped the fiddle and hid it in the bulrushes.

My great-granddaddy Crook was wounded in the Civil War. After recovering, he was assigned to a different regiment than he originally had served with, so he just went AWOL and rejoined his original regiment. At the end of the war, he had to hitchhike from Yankee territory back to Georgia.

Arry Lee, Leola, and Ellis Crook
Photo courtesy of the Crook family

Our love of Senoia history

My family has long been active in the Senoia Area Historical Society. The historical society's museum has a book of which I also have a copy, *Ah-Ko-Kee American Sovereign*, which was written by Billie Jane McIntosh, the great-granddaughter of Chief William McIntosh. The book tells about her life and that of her grandfather, who sold his land here in Georgia to the government. She tells of Croesy McIntosh, a descendant of William McIntosh. When the Indians were forced to move to Oklahoma on the Trail of Tears, Croesy was taken in by the Bridges family, who lived near Highway 16 on what is now called Luther Bailey Road. She was a young girl at the time and was a servant to them.

As she was some Scotch and mostly Indian, she married a black man and had one son, who became a valet to the Bridges brothers, who were Confederate officers in the Civil War. He contracted smallpox, came home, and was placed in a house behind the main house—called the pest house—and it had a trap door. According to legend, Croesy would slide his food to him, and it is said that she contracted smallpox from him. Today there are two graves on the site of what was once the Bridges homeplace. The graves are just above a pump house the City of Senoia built on the old road, now closed, that ran across to Sugar Hill. The road was on the ridge within shouting distance of Luther Bailey Road inside the Senoia city limits and came back out onto Highway 16 in the vicinity of Quick Street. These two graves are side by side, just off the road prior to reaching the branch at the bottom of the hill. I discovered these graves and surmised them to be the graves of Croesy and her son, as people of their social level were often buried on farm property.

Billie Jane McIntosh published another book titled *From Georgia Tragedy to Oklahoma Frontier*, and it is a biography of Chief Chilly McIntosh, the son of Chief William McIntosh. She has also recently written a biography of Chief William McIntosh that is now available at the History Museum.

Remembering Freeman Sasser

On January 20, 2011, I was asked a question by Mike Massengale about how the Freeman Sasser Building (in the park off Seavy Street by the railroad track) got its name. Mike is a retired gadabout in town who can play you a tune on his mouth harp (harmonica). At one time, his father had a store in the building just north of Senoia City Hall.

My first real recollection of Freeman was at a men's club meeting in the cement block annex behind the Methodist church before it was torn down to build the current attached fellowship building. That night, Freeman, who was known to drink heavily at that time, was extremely inebriated.

Freeman Sasser got a job with Walter Thomas Jewelers in Newnan. He quit the drinking habit, got involved in politics, and later became mayor of Senoia. His political connections secured the property where the tennis courts and Seavy Street city park were located. Then he got the State of Georgia Parks Department to build a swimming pool and bathhouse on this property. After World War II ended, with Freeman's influence, a group of World War I and II veterans—including Roy Shell, Aus Bailey, Eugene Hubbard, Vance Couch, Grady

Couch, Jim Sherman, James Hinesley, and my brother Hugh Crook, who was secretary and treasurer—formed the Senoia Veterans Association. (After the Korean War and Hugh's death, I took over as secretary and treasurer.) Because of his legwork and the many hours he spent on these projects, we veterans named the building the Freeman Sasser Memorial Building.

The building was owned by the Senoia Veterans Association and financed by Newnan Savings and Loan. At one time, we had two notes on the building, a regular note and a balloon note, and were in dire straits as to paying these. At a meeting one night, member P. R. McKnight Sr. said that he would match any money we could raise to pay off the balloon note. We began serving meals in the building on Sunday, with Chicken Q's, ham and potato salad, and other dishes.

I was in charge of boiling tea for these meals in a ten-quart bucket on top of my wife's electric stove at home, and one time I wasn't paying close attention, so the heat on the bottom of the bucket burned the white enamel brown. It cost me a new stove, but I got the tea made.

We still had the main note to be paid on the building, as the members who had pledged payments had fallen by the wayside. I came up with the idea of holding a dance every Saturday night, so I booked teenaged bands from Griffin, Fayetteville, and anywhere else that would play for half the proceeds, which was a dollar per person to get into the dance. Some nights, we had three hundred teenagers from three counties. We called these dances Teen Club, and that is how we paid off the building and retired the note, which we burned in an aluminum pan at our meeting one night.

There was some property in the Freeman estate that was not sold for years out of fear that Mr. Bob Walt's brother Emmett's illegitimate mixed-race son would claim a share of inheritance in said property. Mr. Bob Walt and his wife, Miss Bobbie, had only one child, Mary, who married Byron Mathews, a prominent lawyer in Newnan in his later days, and they had no children. Mr. Mathews' nephew inherited the big tract of land just west of town on Highway 16. We often mused that Mr. Bob Walt was spinning in his grave about this inheritance going out of the Freeman family.

1960 Miss Senoia Area beauty pageant at Senoia pool
Left to Right: Elaine McDaniel, 2nd runner-up;
Eleanor Cooper, winner; Melanie Bedenbaugh, 1st runner-up
Photo courtesy of the estate of Melvin Cheek

Main Street Senoia around 1900
Photo courtesy of Senoia Area Historical Society

Early doctors in Senoia

Early pioneer doctors in Senoia included Dr. A. H. Kemp and Dr. Wilbur Culpepper. Dr. James Tribble came along around 1931 and was with us for years. Then we had a long spell without a doctor until some of us local men decided to recruit a doctor for full-time service. We enticed Dr. Marcos Dones, who had left Puerto Rico and was of Spanish descent, to locate here. He was an MD and DDS. We fixed up offices in the old metal gymnasium on Clark Street for him to practice in rent-free, but Dr. Dones became everybody's friend and did not collect all of his fees, so he had to go to work as a doctor employed by the government. Next we landed Dr. Ivanovic from Serbia, who set up a practice in a house on Johnson Street. He wrote too many narcotics prescriptions without performing full-blown physicals of patients, so the Feds came down on him.

At one time, I served on the board of Coweta General Hospital in Newnan. It was sold because PAPP Clinic and its four surgeons controlled the operation of Coweta General and Newnan Hospital, and we on the board saw a need for more surgeons and specialists in the medical field. Coweta

General was sold to Humana Hospital Corporation with the stipulation that they build an office building next to Coweta General and bring in more doctors to break the dynasty of PAPP Clinic. I have lived long enough to see Piedmont build a new hospital, take over what was Coweta General, buy PAPP Clinic, and build a great new hospital on Poplar Road with a million-plus-dollar contribution from the dissolved Newnan Hospital Foundation. Many of the doctors in this part of the county work under the umbrella of Piedmont Healthcare, which handles the bookwork and medical records. Now we have two clinics in uptown Senoia and another at the western city limits in a strip center there.

Sugar Hill (which starts at Bobby Hatchett's old service station building on Highway 16 across from Crook's Marketplace and goes south) is a ridge of land that runs across and down into the branch on Luther Bailey Road. Just before the branch is a cement block building that was a pump house for a City of Senoia well. This is where the road that ran across the ridge came out onto Luther Bailey Road from Highway 16.

On this ridge lived several black families, including the family of Alvin Chunn, who worked on the railroad, probably under the supervision of Mr. Albert Duke, the grandfather of Sonny Duke. At the next house along the ridge lived Harmon Vincent, a black man who was a volunteer on the wooden fire wagon that was pulled by the bumper on the rear of a pickup truck. At the next house before the road turned downhill to Luther Bailey Road lived a black woman named Feebie who had some beautiful flowers around her house when she lived there in the early 1930s.

Friends with Ellis Crook, at right
Photo courtesy of the Crook family

The Stone Lodge at Marimac Lakes

I was once asked about the rock lodge at the head of the city park where the library is located. Well, the rock came from the old duck mill, which was located across the railroad at the south end of Bridge Street and was set up to produce overalls prior to the Great Depression, but the mill was never operated.

My father hired out his team of mules and wagon to move these rocks to the location at the head of Marimac Lake, as it was known when Mr. Carl McKnight built it. (This Carl McKnight is the brother of the present Carl McKnight's grandfather.) A pair of mules pulled the big scoop bucket that dug the dirt out, and this is where my father, A. L. Crook, hired out his team and laborers.

Years ago, Mr. Lee Hutchinson, the father of J. B. Hutchinson Sr. and the grandfather of J. B. Hutchinson Jr. (Jimmy), had a cabin on Keg Creek, just below the dam on Rockaway Road. He hosted young boys from the Sunday school class that he taught, and he could have been one of the early pioneers of Boy Scouting in Senoia. Mr. Walt Arnall and Mr. Lee Hutchinson were the owners of Senoia Hardware when World War II came along. Mr. J. B. Hutchinson had the Ford automobile dealership prior to World War II, and when the war started and no cars were built, Jeeps and Army vehicles were built instead. Hardware was scarce, so Mr. Lee and Mr. Walt decided to close shop, and Mr. J. B. Hutchinson moved the inventory from across the street into the car dealership building.

When the war ended, Mr. J. B. was able to get about three or four cars in to sell, and the first one, a 1946 Ford, was sold to Mr. George El (G. E.) Morgan, who lived at the corner of Johnson Street and Main Street. Then, to the surprise of Mr. J. B., Ford Motor Company demanded that he remove the hardware he had accumulated and was selling and remodel and modernize his showroom to feature their cars. But they couldn't guarantee regular delivery of autos right after the war, so Mr. J. B. said no, and that was the end of Hutchinson Motor Company and the real beginning of Hutchinson Hardware. Mr. J. B. also questioned whether he could sell enough cars in Senoia, so Ford closed the dealership.

Mr. J. B. also had the distributorship of Standard Oil Company during World War II, and of course, sales were limited, as gas was rationed and very little of it was available. Then, about 1950, Standard Oil changed the dealership of their products to a dealer in Newnan. Mr. J. B. applied for and got a better deal with Gulf Oil.

Remember, my dad had made a deal with Mr. J. B. about

selling his gas, and since my father had tuberculosis and had been in bed for two years, I was running the gas station. Mr. J. B. took me to Standard Oil headquarters in Atlanta and had me march in and tell them I was operating the station. Since I was a minor, they had no contract with me, therefore they needed to remove their pumps and equipment. The next week, we were selling Gulf gas with Mr. J. B. as our distributor.

When Mr. J. B. Sr. drowned in the lake on Rockaway Road, his son Jimmy had to come home from the University of Georgia and take over the business. He was about twenty-one years old. He started by driving the gas truck for deliveries to the service stations, but my dad told him to go back uptown to look after the hardware store and the books (and watch the till), and hire someone to drive the gas delivery truck, so he did.

I loved Jimmy like a brother, but he was not good at collecting the money people owed him. One of the stations he supplied went out of business still owing him for gas when they should have been paying on a cash-up-front basis. I also taught him how to process his collections paperwork through the justice of the peace court and put the rendered judgment on record at the courthouse.

When this bankrupt gas dealer started to sell his property, there sat Jimmy's lien on the property. The man threatened Jimmy to make him take the lien off the record at the courthouse. Jimmy called me and I told him to sit tight, that they had to pay him before they could get a clear deed to the property, which they eventually did.

Law and order

Alvin Chunn's son A. C. and his wife, Emma, had three children: Junior, Robert, and Anthony. One night, A. C. became intoxicated, and he was going to shoot Emma. Robert, who had served in the military, came to his mother's defense and grabbed another gun and killed his father. My father told Sheriff Lamar Potts that it was self-defense, and no further investigation was necessary. This investigation (or lack thereof) was quite different from the way such an incident would be handled today.

My recollection is that the first policeman in Senoia was Bose Cooper, the father of former Senoia mayor Johnny Cooper. Next, along came Mr. George Welden, whom we called Creepin' Jesus, as he had no automobile and had to drag offenders to jail if they were too drunk to walk home. Then along came Carl Drake, a night watchman with a punch clock who stopped by each merchant's door. He would take a key out of a box and turn it in his clock to prove what time he'd come by.

Then came Mr. J. Adcock, the father of Bobby Adcock, who played for the Newnan Browns baseball team. He was followed by his brother, John Wallace Adcock, who became a famous basketball coach in Alabama and is also in the Coweta County Sports Hall of Fame. Later, we had a policeman who was fired after being caught having sex with an inmate in the jail (back when it was located in the old city hall).

I later hired a policeman from Griffin, Marshall Ledbetter, to chaperon a dance sponsored by the American Legion. He became embroiled in a fight with a black man he was arresting and the black man broke both Marshall's arms, and a civil riot nearly broke out. Jimmy Hutchinson, then about twenty-five, was mayor, and he stood in the middle of the street and made the white contingent stay on one side of the street uptown and the black contingent stay on the opposite side of the street until the county sheriff's department rolled in. Jimmy had played football at Newnan High School and was a sturdily built young man you would not have wanted to tackle. He was the youngest mayor that anyone can remember holding that office and the youngest mayor in Georgia at that time.

When Billy Roesel was mayor, the joke was that they hired a policeman who fit the uniform they had on hand, as they were operating on a thin budget.

Those days were quite a change from all the police cars and professional police we have today.

Colorful characters I have known

A true anecdote that I have been told concerns W. B. (Doc) Tinsley—the father of William, Roy, Katherine, Lucy, Jerry, and Patsy—and C. H. Cleveland—the father of (Big) Nerine, Libby, Joyce (Smith), Parker (Sr.), J. W., and Jane.

C. H. (Clarence) Cleveland encountered Doc one day coming by the Central of Georgia depot. C. H. saw the diamond ring Doc was wearing, and it being quite ostentatious, C. H. inquired about the ring and asked Doc how much he would take for it. They agreed upon the price, and C. H. purchased the ring. The next time his wife, Dovie, drove him to Newnan, he took it to a jeweler to see if he'd gotten a good deal. The jeweler looked at the ring and immediately saw it was a zircon—a fake.

C. H. took his medicine quietly. One day, Doc came driving by, and C. H. flagged him down and said, "I have a mule in my barn over at the house, and I have no need for him. How much will you give me for the mule?" Mules were bringing a pretty good price in those days, so Doc popped off a number, and C. H. took him up on it.

Doc said, "I'll send William over to get the mule." When

William got there, the mule was dead, so the last laugh was on Doc.

Mr. Edwin A. Cheek, whose picture hangs in the Senoia Area Historical Society's headquarters house (now the Senoia Area Historical Museum), was a carpenter at one time and a person who never spoke ill against anybody. He could play a tune with a leaf from a tree and also with a handsaw. Ray Sewell got Mr. Cheek to do some work on his house one day, and after Mr. Cheek was finished, Ray asked how much he owed. Mr. Cheek told him the price. Ray, hoping to see Mr. Cheek get angry or upset, joked that this was too much, to which Mr. Cheek calmly replied, "Well, that's my price." Ray Sewell saw then, as he already knew, that Mr. Cheek, a man of quiet and honorable disposition, could not be disturbed. He was another of Senoia's great persons of character.

Postmistress Etta Arnall and employee Susie Sullivan in Senoia Post Office, Photo courtesy of Senoia Area Historical Society

Senoia had a postmistress in the 1930s by the name of Mrs. Etta Arnall, who was the grandmother of Frank ("Buddy") Hollberg II. She and Mrs. Susie Sullivan were the two who ran the post office. Miss Etta kept an ironclad control on the mail carriers. She wore her hair in a bun on the back of her head and walked with authority.

Dr. James Tribble came to Senoia around 1931. He, Dr. Wilbur Culpepper—who lived in the Culpepper house at the corner of Broad Street and Morgan Street's southeast corner—and a young nurse named Rachael Bedenbaugh Whittington were in attendance when I was delivered. I was born on June 1, 1931, in a house, now long gone, at the entrance to Tinsley Way. I apparently did not want to enter this world, so Dr. Tribble placed a set of forceps around my head and pulled me out. Over the years, he often felt of my head and wondered with amazement that he did not injure me for life.

Dr. Tribble would see patients while the front door of his office was standing wide open. He regularly prescribed castor oil and some other laxatives, I guess figuring if you had a stomach bug, you'd get rid of it real quick with any of those medicines. If someone was real sick, he would tell you in front of God and everybody—and the open door to the street—to drop your drawers, then he would use a big needle to give you 500 cc of penicillin. Patients would get well real soon—or at least never come back for another shot.

In the mid-1950s, Dr. Tribble, M. H. Elder Jr., and I were the only Senoia members of the Elks Club in Newnan. M. H. had been a member in Atlanta before moving his membership. Dr. Tribble became a member so he could buy his spirits in bottles from the bar. I became a member so I could dance and party (which I still like to do). This was about six years prior to my marriage, but I kept my membership even after that.

One evening, M. H. Elder Jr. staged a "This is Your Life" presentation about Dr. Tribble at East Coweta High School. The word spread prior to that night, and the auditorium was filled with family and people that Doc had delivered and cared for his whole career. His sister had even flown down from New York. The event was quite a surprise for him, and he was a real sport that night.

I must tell you about the time the tinker mechanic "Doc" Tinsley took an A-model Ford chassis and put a Franklin air-cooled engine on the back of the frame. He also had an airplane propeller attached, a wooden box up front to sit in, and an open-air seat behind the steering wheel. To uptown Senoia he came. Dirt streets were all we had in those days, and he was blowing dust everywhere. As he passed the millinery shop, one of the old maid Sims sisters, Miss Sack, stepped outside, and he blew her wig off. (Prior to that, nobody

"Doc" Tinsley driving his aircar
Photo courtesy of Senoia Area Historical Society

knew Miss Sack wore a wig, but the whole town knew now.) If you tried a stunt like that today, they would put you in the crazy house.

Another time, Doc, being the clown he was, took his whole family uptown to Swain Peeples' café one day to have some fun. He'd brought along a dozen or more eggs from the hen-house, and he borrowed Swain's stove and kettle-boiled the eggs. He did buy a loaf of bread, but he then used the café's mustard and mayonnaise to make egg sandwiches for his family, just to prove a point about how much of a person's goodwill you can use up before they kick you out. In later years, Doc's daughter Katherine and her husband, Harold Awtry owned and operated the Pineview Grill, which was located at the same spot where the new orange Mexican restaurant is now on the corner of Highway 85 and 16. I wonder if anyone ever came in their restaurant and did the same thing.

The story goes that the revenuers were at Doc's place one day on a tip and were furiously searching for contraband (untaxed) liquor. Doc teased them about how close they were to locating said spirits (saying "Warmer!" and "Colder!"), but they never did find them. According to local gossip, the spirits were stashed inside the water tower that sat in his yard.

There was a local bridge club started in the 1930s that was, at the time, made up of Senoia society ladies who lived on Pylant Street, including Miss Mary McKnight, Mrs. Rowe (her sister), Mrs. Maude Atkinson, Miss Janie Hunter (the wife of J. D. Hunter), Mrs. Frank (Mamie) Blount, and Mrs. C. H. (Dovie) Cleveland.

Dovie Cleveland—and later, her daughters—drove a 1941 DeSoto automobile. I was the same general age as some of the daughters and remember going to her house to visit them. Miss Dovie would roll back the rug in the music room so we could dance, and she would serve us Coca-Cola.

Miss Dovie's daughter Joyce Cleveland Smith lives in an antebellum home on Bridge Street, which has been on the Senoia tour of homes many times. Joyce Smith's father worked in the train depot that used to be at the bottom of Main Street. Unfortunately, the family doesn't have any pictures of Mr. Cleveland at the depot or even pictures of the depot itself. If any readers have access to such photos, please contact the Senoia Area Historical Society so the pictures can be shared with the family while also being preserved in our local museum.

Prior to Bill and Joyce's purchase of this home quite a number of years ago, Meyer and Carrie Lou Goldberg (the daughter of Mr. Jim Couch of Couch's Hill) resided here. Mr. Meyer Goldberg was a silk-stocking lawyer in Newnan in the 1930s and early 1940s.

C. F. Hollberg Sr. was mayor around 1944, and a small business opened up on Highway 16 and sold groceries from 8 to 9:30 a.m. on Sunday morning and then from about 1 to 6 p.m. in the evening. The mayor also sold groceries in the back of one of his stores, so he enacted the blue laws that said no groceries could be sold on Sunday. This was quite a reaction, but without enforcement, it soon was forgotten. Hollberg's in those days had a drugstore, hardware store, and dry goods and grocery combination. J. P. Brown and Bill Williams were two of their outstanding employees who kept the stores progressing.

Behind the new four-story building built downtown in 2008 is a concrete-and-grass parking lot (located behind Maguire's pub in 2019), where Uncle D. Hunter operated a livery barn where traveling "drummers" could leave their horses while spending the night at the Hollberg Hotel (now The Veranda Bed and Breakfast). These drummers called on quite a number of stores in town, peddling their merchandise. According to legend and observation, Uncle D. chewed chewing gum quite a bit, and it was said he was so tight with his money that he would save the wrapper from the gum and, at the end of the day, put the gum back in the wrapper and save it for the next day's chewing.

Later, Mr. Otis Lindsay operated a building supply and house-building headquarters from an office in the barn. He sold concrete blocks after World War II. His country home is an antebellum house at the corner of Highway 74 and Redwine Road and was recently used as a doctor's office.

Mr. Harvey Thurmond was a rural mail carrier in the 1920s, and he owned a home and land at the corner of

Tinsley Way and Highway 16. He also owned all the land from the Atlantic Coast Line Railroad past the intersection of Highway 85 going toward Griffin. Doc Tinsley bought all the land in this area from Harvey's widow, Mattie Thurmond. When Georgia 85 came through, Doc owned all the land around this intersection.

His son Roy ended up purchasing all the land on the south side of Highway 16 down to and including land he built the airport upon from the Frank Daniel Estate. This made him my across-the-road neighbor. Roy and Mary Louise Brown Tinsley had five children—Angela, Mike, Wayne Barry, Gloria, and Margaret. The three youngest children were close in age to my own, and they attended school together, waiting at the end of my driveway for the school bus.

Wayne Barry was a Tinsley through and through—as was the case with most of his Tinsley relatives, there wasn't anything with an engine or wheels that he couldn't operate or fix. Roy Tinsley had taken his family down to Carrabelle, Florida, to look at buying a single-engine plane. The owner and Wayne took it for a test flight, and sadly, the family watched the plane descend and crash. Wayne had recently graduated high school and was engaged to be married. He had even built a small brick house for his bride directly in the "V" of Highway 16 and Chestlehurst Road. Wayne and my son Ken were great buddies, and both have gone to join their heavenly father.

Life lessons I have learned

As a young man, I overheard a conversation that happened at the Senoia United Methodist Church. One Sunday morning as two men conversed, one noticed the hat the other had on and asked where the man had bought the hat. The man replied, "From Bill Addy at C. P. Daniel," and the other said, "I bought mine from Oscar Brown," at which time the latter asked the first how much he had paid, as both hats were identical. It turned out one man had paid $5.95 while the other had paid $4.95. With little money to be had in those days, the overcharged man was plunged into a fit of anger.

I learned early on to make the price of an item the same for everyone. I didn't care if they were millionaires, they paid just as much as the guy with limited income. I proved that to two big-feeling persons this past year, one a millionaire and the other an airline pilot. I did not sell them tires, but I didn't compromise my principles. You see, I came out of the cotton patch, and my money was limited and scarce, so my money should have just as strong purchasing power as theirs.

While I was attending the Brantley Institute on Clark

Street in Senoia and living on the farm, a nickel was gold, but I had a buddy named Eddie Stephens who would pick up a quarter or two while working on cars for Doc Tinsley. Eddie was an orphan who lived about a mile from my house with Doc, who was his uncle. I walked home with him, as he lived on Dolly Nixon Road, past our house. Eddie made a few coins working on automobiles at Doc's junkyard, and we would sometimes stop by Addy's Grocery, where Eddie would buy a Pepsi-Cola and a pack of peanuts, pour the peanuts into the Pepsi, and we would both swig off that one drink while we walked home. I had no money, as we were dirt farmers living on Luther Bailey Road. Today, Luther Bailey's fourth generation is living on the old homeplace. Charles Bailey and his sister, Ann Bailey, live there now. Charles was in the nursery and landscaping business, and Ann is a retired nurse.

It's amazing that the child that you encounter on his way up could be the one who helps you on your way down in life. This is true of the Addy sisters, Kate and Isadore, who were famous for their hot dogs and sold them downtown in Senoia for many years. They were my mother's double first cousins and relatively wealthy by Senoia standards, as they worked hard and never spent money on frivolous items. (They also never handed out free hot dogs, either, and free was the only price I could afford as a boy.) When they became the only remaining siblings still living in their family homeplace, located on one hundred acres on Standing Rock Road, Kate (the younger but more able sister) had to have surgery, and she signed an unlimited power of attorney over to her nephew. While she was in the hospital, Isadore was placed by their nephew at Brightmoor Nursing Center in Griffin, and Kate went there to recuperate after her surgery. In a few months, Kate started getting better, and they talked of moving back home.

Shortly after that, their nephew took them to see their home for the day. Soon after they left that same day, the house caught on fire and burned. It was interesting that the nephew had already transferred the property title to himself and increased the value of the insurance. After the house burned, they had no home to ever return to again. I would send cookies and "Irish" potato chips and other treats to the nursing home, and my sister, Edith Crook Sewell, took them goodies as well as cake on their birthdays. Kate lived to be ninety-two years old, and Isadore lived to be one hundred and three years old, but both ended up living in that nursing home for over twenty years with a twenty-five-dollar-a-month allowance until their deaths.

Ellis Crook at the piano
Photo courtesy of the Crook family

A hip-pocket financier

I was born at the home on Highway 16 that is located diagonally across from the east corner of property I have owned since 1965, now the entrance to Tinsley Way. At that time, I swapped my dad's property on the left prior to going up Couch's Hill just west of our supermarket because the lot would not give me proper egress, and I couldn't buy the adjacent lot. Across the road was a house built by Reverend Whitley, a Baptist preacher, and his brother which is located at the base of Couch's Hill. This is where my wife, Pat, and I first lived after we married and the home to which we brought my daughter, Cheryl, after she was born. It had central air-conditioning—if you put a box fan in the middle of the house.

By the time I was eighteen, I was buying autos at Bishop Brothers Auction on Stewart Avenue in Atlanta. A lot of cars had been stored during World War II and were now being sold since the war was over. One night, I bought a 1936 Ford and found out on the way home that the back floorboard had rusted out due to Yankees putting salt on their roads.

I was a hip-pocket financier with a cowboy hat and a big

leather pocketbook with a chain, which I used to carry my money and notes of those who owed me for the autos. I needed some money to go back to the sale for more autos, and I went to Mr. Bob Walt Freeman at Farmers and Merchants Bank, in the original location, to sell him two notes I had on two cars I had sold. He said he would take the notes and give me money for them "with recourse," which sounded like a good deal to me. But I did not realize that the cars were going to be wrecked and there was no insurance on them. I had a tough time paying off those notes, but I never forgot what the words "with recourse" meant. I sold autos and worked at the store until Uncle Sam got me in 1952.

I received several deferments to keep the business operating, but the draft finally caught up with me, and I was inducted on May 15, 1952. Thank goodness Dad was able to come down to the store to sit in a chair and watch over the store because not all the employees were honest. One of the employees had bought a set of tires from Gordy Tire Company that he had charged to the store but were on his auto. Dad could not prove this, but it made him angry, so the employee had to go. Dad was lucky that he had recovered enough to mind the store and hold on to the business.

I spent two years in the Army, of which the best part was the nightlife in the town of Columbia, South Carolina. After basic training, I joined three other guys in renting an apartment just back of the University of South Carolina, and

I developed quite a little black book. I had a lot of good times, and that was where I saw my first drive-in hamburger parlor with girls in short shorts hopping the cars. The name of the drive-in was Doug Broome's.

I was sent to radio school after basic training to learn the international Morse code, and I barely passed or was forced to pass, and I came out with orders to FECOM (Far East Command-Korea). I was lucky that I ran into a guy I went to school with in Atlanta, and he asked if I could type. I said yes, so he put me in for Officer Candidate School to keep me from shipping out, and then he transferred me to the officers' record section at regimental personnel. My job was to type up the chronological duty stations of officers—without mistakes. I wish I'd had a computer then.

Upon my discharge on May 15, 1954, I returned to Senoia and began work in the store. I enrolled at Georgia State in downtown Atlanta as a special student. I knew that I might never be able to finish, so I took select subjects that I knew I would need in the business world, and I have approximately ninety credit hours at Georgia State.

While I was gone from the store, my dad had hired a Mr. Lassiter from Newnan, and I remember very vividly the scene I saw when I walked into the store upon being discharged from the Army. Mr. Lassiter had his foot propped on the back of the meat case and was looking out toward the front door. Joe Watson, the brother of longtime employee

John Alvin, was working for Dad, and he was lying across the drink box up in the front window. Dad was sitting in a chair. I said to myself, "Somebody has to wake this place up." To this day, I can't stand watching people sit around while there's work to do.

Later, Dad hired Howell Cook as a meat cutter, and he once got disgusted with me for asking him to do something and said, "You think you're a G.D. second lieutenant." He had served in the Marines. Howell later became our competitor by opening a grocery store in what became the repair shop side of Bobby Hatchett's station.

Howell could paint signs real well, and he hung them on his glass storefront. I learned rather quickly to paint signs and, for my grocery signs, used the old swinging-on-a-stand Gulf sign, where you were supposed to advertise their monthly features, so that I could compete fiercely with Howell's prices. If you will look inside our gas station at the picture of me, the one taken in front of the store we tore down, you can see some of my sign painting.

While Bobby Hatchett is on my mind, he operated one of the only two "full service" stations that Senoia has ever had. Roy Tinsley owned the other one at the corner of Highway 16 and 85. After self-service gasoline (which was cheaper) came about, Bobby Hatchett began his welding business, and he welded all the bar joists in the supermarket I built and opened in 1981. Bobby and I have been business people down on Highway 16 for over forty years, never had a cross word, and have always had the highest regard for one another.

Ellis and Patricia Yarbrough Crook with children, Cheryl, Ken, and Greg
Photo courtesy of the Crook family

Ellis Crook at the meat counter of Crook's Food Mart
Photo courtesy of the Crook family

Buying the store from Dad

Around 1959, I was brainwashed by a meat cutter by the name of Major Green to furnish my money for us to go into business together in Griffin as partners—using my money, of which I did not have enough, and his talent to take one-half of the profit. But my brother Alva intervened, thank goodness. He carried me down to Thomas Packing Company in Griffin and had Frank Thomas try to talk some sense into my head, then Alva convinced my dad, who was then in his seventies, to sell out to me and let me pay him for the business and rent the building so I would have something to do.

In January of 1960, I signed a note for the inventory in the building and started paying Dad one hundred dollars a week. I also provided all the groceries he needed and a stipend until he died. I got married on July 10, 1960, and with Pat teaching school, we were able to pay Dad that one hundred dollars a week. Within three years, we had him paid off and never borrowed another penny from him.

We had the first cash register in Senoia that spilled the customer's change into a cup when it totaled the sale. In later years, I installed the first air-conditioning in a store in Senoia, bought new refrigerator cases, and put in metal shelves. I took the old wooden shelves to Alabama and put them in the store belonging to my father-in-law. The first frozen food sold in Senoia was from a six-foot case I had. Cold coils appeared every foot, with aluminum covers that collected ice or frost, and every two or three days, they had to be removed and the ice washed from them. Birds Eye was one of the first brands I remember carrying. I had to pick up dry ice on Moreland Avenue then go out just past the East Lake Country Club to my brother Alva's grocery store to pick up the frozen food. I transported it in a two-wheel trailer using two non-working home refrigerators (packed with dry ice, basically serving as our coolers), and that was how the first frozen food was delivered to Senoia.

During his operation of the store, my dad had constructed two twenty-five-foot additions on the east side of the building and a feed room on the west side. Later, he added about twenty feet onto the rear of the building. The electrical main was originally installed by Luke Hunnicutt, the grandfather of Mike Hunnicutt, who in later years worked in the supermarket. It was a 60-amp main, but later a 100-amp main was installed, and then later a 200-amp main was installed. By the time I added air-conditioning, new meat cases, a new dairy case, and a new produce case, Ferrell Parrott, who was doing electrical work around 1965, added a 500-amp three-phase main so that we finally did not have overheated breakers in the electrical switches.

When Crook's Marketplace was built, a contract was signed between R. O. Jones of Newnan Oil Company and me to install self-service pumps and a canopy plus three eight-thousand-gallon tanks, with the profit split between the two of us. Later, I negotiated a deal for Mr. Jones to sell the property he owned across the street to Bank of Coweta (now Synovus). That was the last thing he was able to do, as he died two days after signing the deed.

After Mr. Jones' death, I exercised my right to buy out my contract with Newnan Oil Company at its depreciated price and had complete control of gasoline purchases and the retail price of gas. That was the sweetest deal I ever pulled, as I got a bank for a neighbor and avoided any gas station competition. We were the first store with air-conditioning, the first supermarket with the first automatic doors in Senoia, the first tire center, the first finance company, and one of the first self-serve gas stations.

We also had the first legal used car lot in town, Peach State Auto Sales and Leasing, Inc., which began with John Thompson, my son-in-law, as the original operator.

Dad always tried to improve the bank account. He bought three railroad houses that were located on the track just below Clark Street, where the railroad had been built long before I was born. The first house on the east side of Clark was the section foreman's, and the next three were lived in by section hands who worked on the railway. While I was going to grammar school, the first house was the home of Talmadge McKnight and his wife. Talmadge McKnight sold and transported moonshine, as it was hard to make a living in those days of the Great Depression. The three houses just south of where Talmadge lived were the three that Dad bought, and he moved two of them to the east side of Bridge Street just before you get to the Atlantic Coast Line Railroad. Dad later sold one to Willie James Stafford, who worked on the railroad and had plowed for Dad prior to going to work for the railroad.

John Drake, the local black carpenter, lived in the house next to where Dad later sold a lot to Albert Alexander, a black man who worked for and retired from Delta Air Lines. It was hard for black people to be able to obtain property.

Talmadge McKnight's brother was Jewel McKnight, whose wife, Mabel, worked at Southern Mills. We used to joke that Jewel was a real go-getter: he would take his wife to work every day and then "go get her" after work.

Gerald McKnight, also the son of Jewel McKnight, had five children—Tim, Wayne, Stanley, Rhonda, and Vera—and three of them worked with me. They were the best-raised and most well-mannered workers, and today they continue to look after each other and are always willing to help each other—a remarkable trait inherited from a big family.

Talmadge McKnight had to quit bootlegging moonshine

because he couldn't make enough money to pay off Senoia Chief of Police Marshall Ledbetter when he came to town and keep paying Coweta County Sheriff Lamar Potts' satchel man, J. H. Potts, who collected the kickbacks.

Sheriffs back then could not send their daughters to college, live in a nice home, and pay their bills with the small salary paid by the county. The salaries have improved, thank goodness, because with the media exposure, now you could not get by with what the sheriffs did for years.

Before and after photos of latest downtown Senoia city improvements
Photo courtesy of Stephen Sweet

Making change in changing times

I made extra money by loaning money. When I bought my dad out in 1960, I ordered the latest machine from National Cash Register. It let you ring up groceries by department, and it had a posting key to add balances to accounts, a slide table on the side to place the ledger card for posting charges, and an automatic change maker that dispensed the coins. People came by to see the coin dispenser in action. I paid over three thousand dollars by monthly payments for that cash register.

Dad thought I had lost my mind, as I owed him fifteen thousand dollars, and I reckon he was worried I might not be able to pay him. I wanted to be able to track my profits, sales, and sales tax. A 3 percent sales tax was passed in 1951 while Herman Talmadge was governor. We figured the tax in our heads and put our money in the drawer. We put the sales tax in a jar by the register so we would not pay the state more than we took in. Try putting a jar by the register today and see how long it lasts. When he was a teenager and worked for us, Allyn Bell figured the tax in his head. Can teenagers do this now?

As time progressed, I placed a three-foot-by-three-foot piece of fiberboard on top of one of the grocery buggies, and that became the "desk" where I made out notes when I loaned money. I would post the loan to a ledger card with the same type register that I had bought earlier, the National 6000, of which I had purchased two more.

In 1973, the economy was bad, and I had these pilots' wives and others who spent their allotted grocery money on pleasure items and stalled on paying their grocery bills. So I sent out a letter that February stating that all balances owed in our files every Monday morning would have a 2 percent service charge added to the account. Well, I got those delinquent customers out of the way and kept the blue-collar worker (who paid on time), and at the end of 52 weeks had most of my money regularly paid back on time with the service-charge option for those who wanted to carry a balance (and pay the extra 2 percent on the balance each week).

I bought a 10-by-30-foot house trailer and placed it on the west side of the gas station.

The trailer was placed there around 1970 for use as an office. Jean Shell moved into this office for bookkeeping, and she worked for me for over thirty years. She and I wrote checks, paid bills, and processed our court papers so we could collect money people owed. Later on, I used this trailer for a game room, where mostly younger customers paid to play video games. We split the take with the owner of the video games. My sons took this money and bought a used boat that we pulled to the lake with our station wagon, but because the station wagon was loaded down and was also towing a boat, it usually overheated, making for memorable family trips.

The trailer's septic tank was covered over when Dad built onto the rear of the store, so there was nowhere to place the sewage line from the trailer. I buried two 55-gallon barrels in the ground and ran my sewage pipe from the trailer into them. Of course, down the road I had—and have always had—sewage problems, even at the supermarket, because there was not enough property to run in-ground drain lines. From 2002 until the city got sewerage, I had to haul excess water from the supermarket's second septic tank to dispose on my own property. I called my truck "the honey bucket."

Back in the 1960s and 1970s, all carbonated beverages were sold in glass bottles, which you could return for a 5-cent deposit per bottle. We would take in car trunk or truck bed loads of bottles and have to sort them according to the company—Coke, Pepsi, RC Cola. We had a "bottle pile" out behind the store, and I usually made my son Ken sort the bottles for a few hours on Saturdays, which he did not like. One day, my meat market manager stepped outside for a smoke, and he saw Ken, who would have been around eight years old at the time, tossing bottles and smashing them. He got in a lot of trouble that day because every bottle he smashed was worth a nickel, which added up quickly. My money was always short, but one day I heard the deposit on glass Coca-Cola bottles was going from five cents to ten cents, so I started sending the Coke-product bottles all down to my house and stacking them in the field, not letting the drivers pick them up every week. When the deposit went up to ten cents, I had the Coca-Cola Company pick them up, and a convoy of trucks hauled them back. I made enough off that venture to put a new tile floor in the store.

Grand opening photos of new updated Crook's Marketplace
Photos courtesy of the Crook family

Planning a new supermarket

John Waters, my meat market manager of over thirty years, kept pushing me to build a supermarket. I undoubtedly ate too much ego food, so I began having the co-op in Atlanta draw up floor plans for a new store. I also began to go to auctions where supermarket chains were closing down and bought pieces of equipment that would fit my floor plan. To store this equipment, I rented a warehouse in Newnan from Joe Crain.

The equipment was stored there for over two years while I tried to get a good set of plans drawn for the building. The property on which I was going to build the supermarket was purchased from three different landowners. One of them was Render Gresham, who inherited the land from his wife, Ruth Estes Gresham, who was deceased. She was the daughter of Nat Estes and, due to the number of children in the family, was raised by three old maids who lived diagonally across the street from her mother and father. Ruth's brother was Bill Estes of Haralson, who took over his father-in-law's big farms when he married Louise, the daughter of Mr. Otto Hutchinson, who co-owned the big store there with Mr.

McGahee. It was called the Hutchinson-McGahee General Merchandise Store. The three old maids were Miss Jimma, Miss Sack, and Miss Nan.

I finally got the plans drawn by a draftsman who worked for the Big Apple food chain. His brother, a certified engineer, put his seal on the plans so I could take them to loaning institutions to borrow the money. I had served on the board of Coweta General Hospital with the president of Newnan Federal Savings & Loan. Pat had some money she had inherited from her father that was already at the bank. I had told the bank president of my plan. This man said when I got ready, to come and see him.

In 1980 with Jimmy Carter as president, the interest rate was climbing, so the bank president undoubtedly saw a chance to make big interest by placing the bank's money in fed funds, or else he didn't want to take a chance on me. He suggested I go to the Farmers Home Administration, the Small Business Administration, and I washed my drawers to everyone while trying to borrow money. I had let the contract on faith that I was going to get the money, and the walls were going up. I was tossing in bed all night and worrying all day about how I was going to survive because I was going to run out of money with an incomplete building.

Having served on the hospital board, I knew about the Coweta County Industrial Development Authority, and I began to contact the chairman of the board and the secretary,

Julian (G-Boy) Roberts of Haralson. I knew everyone on the board, and they said they would authorize the tax-exempt status of the bonds if I had them issued.

My next step was to get a lawyer to begin the paperwork, and since I'd served on the hospital board with Charlie Mottola, the county attorney, he said he could do so. He drew up the paperwork, for which I paid his firm four thousand dollars, then I paid the bond attorney in Atlanta four thousand dollars. Then the problem was to get some financial institution to buy the bonds.

While on the hospital board, I had also gotten to know Harold Hammond, the president of First National Bank. He said that his son, who called himself a financial advisor, could legally take eight thousand dollars cash of my money to get the bank—run by his father—to buy the bonds with the bank's money, which was a total of $425,000. I paid this amount back at the rate of $4,200 a month and had an electric bill of $5,000 a month plus payroll, and I felt like I was laced in a straitjacket for a long time.

A Georgia Power representative would not let me mail the payment for my electric bill. They would come and pick it up, as they thought I was going to fall on my behind. A lot of days, I thought so also, but with John Waters knowing how to run the meat market and make money, I survived the lean years, as the store was too big for the area at the time it opened on August 26, 1981.

The grand opening was on Wednesday morning, and for the rest of the week, our sales were approximately $40,000. I had already been doing about $25,000 in the old store. I was a disappointed person, and I can still see John Waters' face when I told him the amount of sales in the meat market, as it was in the red. John believed he had done a lot more business than we actually did. I had a farmer who grew produce as my produce manager, and what a mistake that was, as I remember that we threw away many black bananas that were too abundantly ordered.

It was tough times for the next several years, trying to pay back the money that I had borrowed from Farmers and Merchants Bank, as I had mortgaged our home. Because I was not accustomed to operating a large supermarket and the financial strain I was under, I had built up enough cholesterol from stress that I had to have an angioplasty operation in 1983 and a bypass operation a few years later.

Fortunately, better days were ahead.

Crook's enterprises in the modern era

In 1997, my son Greg had plans drawn up for a Colonial design for the current gas station building—Senoia's first modern eight-pump convenience store—along with a suite of offices in the rear for a finance company and insurance agency.

The current tire center sits on a lot that originally contained a cement block building my dad had built in 1949 for a local mechanic named Hiram Todd—the grandfather of Randy, Bill, and Brantly Todd—who rented this cement block building and operated a complete auto, tractor, and truck repair center. Mr. Hiram's wife died when his children—Hiram Jr., Catherine, and Edgar—were real small. His wife's sister, Miss Carrie Lou Booker, a woman of rather large stature, moved in and raised his children. In those days, if you lived with a woman for a certain period of time, she was your common-law wife, and Mr. Hiram got reeled back in every time he tried to date Miss Hattie Shell or Mrs. Daisy Harris (the widow of Homer Harris). Mr. Hiram died in my arms of a heart attack at the tire center on April 10, 1967. He had sold the inventory but had to take the shop back over due to nonpayment of the note by the person he had sold the inventory to upon learning he had a heart condition.

Greg had a metal façade wrapped around the cement block tire center building in 2003 to make it look better next to the new gas station that we had built. But in 2008, the State of Georgia highway department exercised the power of eminent domain to widen Highway 16, and they took our tire center building—and the new metal façade—and paid us what they figured was the value. We finally got them to pay to tear it down.

In 2009, we signed a contract with All Span Builders of Fayetteville to put up a new, more modern tire center with great egress and ingress and a nice waiting room and computers to access inventory and prices. We had some up-to-date computer balancers, tire lifts, and alignment machines, so our inside equipment was a minimal cost compared to the cost of a vacant building and all the equipment to be bought for it.

Along with this new tire center, we built three offices facing Highway 16 at the corner of Bridge Street. We named it the Addy Building after my mother and her people (figuring we had enough of the name "Crook" on the other businesses). The building had to conform to new City of Senoia historical guidelines, which were a challenge, but it looks nice. I also own a house that sits at 104 Bridge Street, directly behind the tire center. This house sat on the same plat of land as the tire center and the commercial building. There was a former mayor who lived on this street, so she deemed the Bridge Street house to be a residential property to prevent me from putting in a parking lot for my businesses.

Bridge Street became closed to all but foot traffic and bicycles when the railroad company deeded the wooden bridge to the City of Senoia, so the railroad does not have to keep this bridge in repair now.

Update begins on Crook's Little Guy location.
Photo courtesy of the Crook family

*Early school photos of Ellis Crook
and Ellis with his parents
Photos courtesy of the Crook family*

Recollections of a childhood in Senoia

I enjoy reminiscing about my childhood. I gave each of my children a picture of me when I was about five years of age, standing in a cotton field with a cotton sack and a straw hat. I told them I'd better see that picture hanging in a prominent place whenever I visited so they would never forget where they came from (and might have to go back to if they didn't work hard). I got a real lesson in sociology and psychology in the cotton field, as I got into a green boll–throwing fight with the other teenagers who had come to help us gather the cotton one afternoon, and they left the field. (A green boll is the hard green boll that later opens up to expose the cotton.) Well, I don't remember whether Dad belted me, but I do remember he kept me in the field until dark and then sent me back early the next day, so I learned to get along with people and get the job accomplished.

As a youngster, I would see the thrashing machine pulling up to the barn, and we had to throw down the bundles of wheat or oats from the loft of the barn so the machine could thrash out the wheat and oats from the hull that hung on the stem of straw. Mr. George Caldwell owned the thrashing machine and was paid either in cash or a portion of the product thrashed. Mr. Caldwell lived on Standing Rock Road and was the father of Elbert Caldwell, whose wife was Montene. After Elbert's death, she married Moody Todd, a widower.

We took the wheat to Elders Mill, located just south of where Rock House Road intersects Elders Mill Road. If we needed cornmeal, it was ground by my grandmother's brother Wes Higgins. He had a small building along the railroad track between Pylant and Main Streets with a water jacket putt-putt engine to drive the grinding wheel.

When I was a teenager, the Irish horse traders (also known as "Travellers") would come to camp in the grove in front of the house I grew up in (the "Candy Bridges" house). They lived in tents with a metal pole outside with two hooks that held large aluminum milk cans. These cans held the water they got from the spigot in our yard. We had city water installed in Senoia in 1937, so this era was a little later.

Their clan was Catholic, and they paid for a priest from Griffin to come hold Mass in the grove on one occasion. "Paddy Boy" Carroll was the nickname of one of the clan's most outstanding characters, and he was quite a horse trader. He had several daughters, including Bridget, who was about my age, Susie, a blonde, and Marie. Dad discouraged me from getting too familiar with Bridget, but I did become a playmate of Jimmy Carroll, whose father was also named

Jimmy. Young Jimmy attended school here in Senoia for a short period while they were camping.

They had no bathroom, and their hygiene was bad. They had trucks with tall bodies and a gate. It took two persons to let down the gate so that the mules could walk up into the truck from which the horse traders toured the country and swapped and sold mules. The women bought linoleum wholesale. They used the two-wheel trailers when they moved their tent and bedding from place to place, and they sold linoleum while their husbands sold mules. You had better measure the 9-by-12 piece before they left, for when it was unrolled, you were likely to have a 9-by-6 piece. They were masters at the game, and that was the reason they could not live anywhere too long, as their reputation would catch up with them.

My dad rented our barn and fenced lot behind the barn to these folks to store mules. Doc Tinsley had a monkey when his family lived on Dolly Nixon Road. One time, the monkey got loose and came up to our place and was riding the backs of the mules in the pen behind the barn. In their confusion and anxiety at having the monkey riding their backs, all the mules got riled up and were about to break out of the pen, so Dad shot Doc's monkey. He figured it would be better to be on Doc's bad side than on that of those "Irishmen."

In 1999, Pat and I went to Charleston, South Carolina, and on the way back, we stopped in Augusta, Georgia, and found the compound that these Irish Travellers had built. They had beautiful homes and their own Catholic church. Some of their family names were Sherlock, Carroll, and Riley. I located Jimmy Carroll, with whom I had played as a kid. He was now an old man, able to travel only a very little, and we also saw Susie, who had become an old white-headed lady.

This group went about with hydraulic presses that they hauled on their pickups and used to paint the roofs on barns. The paint was silver, and it would soon wash off, as it was too thin to stick.

The Irish Travellers married within their clan. Most men were older before they married because they had to have a dowry to give the parents and (usually teenaged) bride-to-be before the wedding. They had the newspapers or reporters onto them about this at one time, so they are careful who they converse with at the compound.

In the late 1930s and perhaps later, they had the funerals of the deceased once a year, and if I remember correctly, they used red caskets.

We had the wooden store building then, and they bought from us at the store. Paddy Boy drank a pint of liquor a day and chewed tobacco constantly, and he still lived to a ripe old age.

We farmed the land where the Bank of Coweta (now Synovus Bank) is located, as at that time it belonged to Mrs. Will Horton, whom I called Hoyt. She lived in the house facing

Luther Bailey Road behind Synovus Bank, and she was my adopted grandmother. We used to dig sweet potatoes after planting the potato slips in rows. When runners began to form off the plants, you had to pick up the runners and lay them longways with the row in order to plow the furrow and keep the grass from taking over the field.

You plowed watermelon vines the same way until they got too big and there were too many runners to move around in order to plow. When we plowed up the sweet potatoes in the fall, Dad would take cornstalks and make a teepee-like structure with pine straw inside on the ground and dirt piled up a good ways outside on the corn stalks, and we stored the sweet potatoes that way in the field.

When we dug Irish potatoes (white potatoes) and onions, we stored them in the loft of the smokehouse. It was my job to put them there, and when Mama needed some, it was also my job to get them down. Picking blackberries in the summer was a thorny job, and I always wanted to keep finding a bigger patch on the edge of the fields along the banks. My mother had a time making me stand in one place and pick blackberries from that spot near her, as I had a tendency to wander off. I never realized at the time that she was watching for snakes.

Kids now need electronic games and gadgets to entertain them, but I had a good time playing in the woods. I used a hatchet to cut small pines, and I made a fort with pine straw for the roof. I remember the hatchet missing once, and I cut my ankle pretty badly. Mother put kerosene on it and wrapped it with a cloth bandage. That was the extent of our "doctoring" back in those days.

Our property and pastures backed up the hill to what we call Sugar Hill, where Alvin Chunn, who worked on the railroad, lived.

A road ran across Sugar Hill and came out where the pump house is located, above the branch just before Dolly Nixon Road begins, and there were about four houses along the ridge where black families lived. Our first black firefighter, Harmon Vincent, lived in one of these houses. Our first fire wagon was a red wagon with rubber tires. The fire wagon had a tongue that you could drop over the bumper of any pickup truck or car and pull to the fire while someone stood on the tongue to keep it from jumping back up off the bumper.

I was assistant fire chief about 1955 and had a siren mounted under the hood of my auto. You volunteered for such positions back then. Nobody got paid for doing these jobs.

Across town, the Coweta Street/Middle Street area was known as Ten Cent Ville. Ray Sewell, my brother-in-law, used city government money to buy Susan Grice's home and move her to a small cement block house in order to get enough property on Ray Street (which was named for him) to build the government housing projects, which are also located on Middle and Johnson Streets.

Mrs. Lucy Sasser, who was the librarian at the old Senoia High School and the mother of Freeman Sasser, was a sister of Bob Walt and Emmett Freeman. Freeman Sasser was a reformed alcoholic who amended his ways and became mayor of Senoia in his later years. Politically, he lobbied the state and got land and a grant to build the swimming pool so that we got the Senoia State Park, which is now Senoia City Park on Seavy Street. Land was bought adjacent to or deeded to the Senoia Veterans Association to build the Legion home adjacent to the park.

The legion building is named the Freeman Sasser Building for all the good works he accomplished for the citizens of Senoia. We used to have beauty contests with the young girls parading around the pool, wearing their swimming attire, where the Scout clubhouse was later located. There were informal beauty contests held, and one girl was chosen as Most Beautiful with several other runners-up.

I got a lot of help in policing the grounds and checking their autos to keep out liquor or beer. There was no crack or marijuana back then, and we didn't have to worry about legal actions as we do today.

James Hindsman, Eugene Hubbard, Billy Roesel, Jim Sherman, and several others helped out on this duty each Saturday night, as I had worked all day in the store and then gone down there to supervise and pay the band their half of the take. I left my young children at home with Pat and was reminded quite often that I was gone too much. Sure enough, when mine got old enough for such good fun, the Teen Club had long since disbanded.

As our membership declined and we no longer had regular meetings, I got as many of them as possible together, and we voted to give the property and building to the City of Senoia with the stipulation that each living member be allowed to use the building at least one day a year and that the city remodel and install a new heating and air system. This was accomplished during the mayoral term of Lester Mann.

I hope the legacy of Freeman Sasser lives on, as in a few years, he made up for what he had missed out on for most of his early adult life and did a great service to Senoia. He had one son who became a doctor but never lived in Senoia.

Wanda Glazier Jones, Bob Caldwell, Jerry Wood, and Bill Tinsley
among dancers and musicians at Teen Club
Photo courtesy of Wanda Glazier Jones

Opening a new business is a gamble

In recent years, I have seen groups boarding the bus in Senoia for a trip to Biloxi, Mississippi, to gamble. Others have made trips to casinos in Cherokee, North Carolina, and also Mississippi. In Senoia in 1954 and for several years thereafter, we had one-armed bandits. They were located here and in Newnan and Griffin in our Veterans, Elks, and Moose Clubs until the Atlanta papers started writing articles that forced the sheriff to close them down.

Speaking of closing down, Senoia has seen a lot of stores closed over the years. Starting at the bottom of the hill on the right, where Senoia Coffee & Café is located, was Nolan's Grocery. Next door was Addy's Grocery, and just up the street, where the Masonic Lodge is located, was the movie theater, then Miss Sack's millinery shop, later Senoia Cleaners. there was a space between the millinery shop and the Senoia post office, originally located in the lower corner of what is now Hollberg's Furniture. Then came Hollberg's Pharmacy, and next door was Hollberg's Dry Goods, with groceries in the rear of that portion of the building. Then was Hollberg's Hardware, then David Park's Barber Shop with a gas station on the corner. Across the street, heading north was Hutchinson's Ford dealership, later a hardware store. Next was Dr. Tribble's office, then Mr. Burnett's shoe shop, and last, Mr. Jones, the father-in-law of Dr. Tribble, had a store in the old wooden building for a short time.

Starting at the bottom of the street on the left side, C. P. Daniel had the lower building for feed and other goods and then the main building for dry goods and groceries in the back. Later, Associated Grocers talked him into putting the groceries up front and making it a Red Dot advertising chain store with the dry goods in back.

Mr. Frank Daniel, the second-generation owner, never did like the grocery business, as they had peach orchards, a cottonseed-oil processing plant in the early 1930s, and a gin in later years. Frank Daniel opened a five-and-dime store where Nic & Norman's is now. Later it became the second location for the Senoia post office, when my brother Hugh was postmaster.

At this time, this second post office building got in such bad shape with the roof leaking that my brother Hugh got Jim Baggarly to build a new post office just under the water tower uptown (where Katie Lou's Café is now). My dad later bought this leaky building and it needed a lot of work, but he didn't have the money or the time to get the roof fixed, and finally, the whole roof caved in. The roof had been suspended by adjacent walls, which were owned by the landowners on each side.

Dad was finally able to sell this location, and the next weekend, the Methodist minister, Dan McFarland, preached on the bad looks of downtown Senoia. He said somebody needed to fix up the buildings. Dad just poked me and grinned, because he didn't own the building anymore.

Just above the ten-cent store and later post office was McKnight's General Merchandise, with a bank pay window in the back, where the office was located along with a walk-in safe. The pay window may have been a holdover from one of the old banks in town. This was the pay window where the McKnights paid the peach pickers and took care of the bills for the gin they owned just below the track down the street.

Next door to McKnight's was Alsie Smith's barbershop, across the street from the movie theater. Alsie was the father of Dorothy Smith Massengale, grandfather of Nancy Massengale Tinsley. Next to that was Haisten Funeral Home's casket office, where Mr. Marlin Haisten—the father of Warren, Ben, and Matt Haisten—held court while his brother Harry ran the Griffin Funeral Home. At one time, they had funeral homes in Jackson, Barnesville, and I believe way back, in Newnan. Later, the sons of Mr. Marlin Haisten ran the funeral homes.

At some point after the funeral home business closed, Tom Harber opened the first pharmacy in Senoia in that building. Going up the street was the original Farmer's and Merchant's bank building. Next door to the bank was Crook & Sewell, a brother and brother-in-law whose partnership in general merchandise terminated when Hugh Crook became postmaster. Then the store became just R. S. Sewell General Merchandise.

Next door beyond them was Cook's Meat Market for some time and, beyond that, the bowling alley. Later, Southern Mills located there after the bowling alley closed.

Across the street on the northwest corner of Seavy and Main was Jake Harwell's Pool Room and short-order restaurant. Next door was Dr. Gardner's dentist office, which was on the left side of the building. In the right side was a restaurant that Swain Peeples operated. Just past the restaurant was the original city hall with the jail in the back, with a police and fire station being built later on the right. (The old city hall was later used as the first site of the Senoia Library and more recently—until the Spring of 2020—it was the Senoia Cycle Works. Currently the old police station is the Welcome Center, and it was previously the second site for the library.) Just above the original police station and current Welcome Center is the building Jim Baggarly built for the post office, as requested by my brother, Hugh. It later was used as a newspaper office and then it became the third site for the Senoia Library until the library moved to its current location on Pylant Street. Now it's Katie Lou's Restaurant.

The old wooden building next to it is the Baggarly building. Here, buggies and wagons were sold during the farming days, with the Coca-Cola plant at one time being at the back in the basement. The present city hall was formerly the 2nd location of Farmers and Merchants Bank.

During World War II, the back part or basement of the Baggarly building (now the Buggy Museum) was used for a canning plant run by George and Susie Welden. Though most cattle were processed by meatpacking companies, calves were killed at home, and the meat was sent to this local canning plant. Food was scarce, and this was a way to have meat on the table for many months to come. The present city hall is where Farmers and Merchants Bank was previously located. Next was Mr. Will Peeks' woodworking shop, where he built wagons from start to finish. On the northwest corner of Main Street, currently occupied by retail shops (with the Baptist church directly behind it), was the main part of his blacksmith shop. I have had to walk mules there in the back where John Dorsey, the father of J. D. Dorsey, who was a little stooped-over black man, shaped the metal shoes and used nails to put them on the hooves of the mules and horses.

According to my mother, the first log cabin in Senoia was located between Baggarly Way and Main Street, diagonally across from the brick church on Main Street (where a parking lot is now). That is where the Indian trail called McIntosh Trail came through Senoia, headed from Indian Springs to the bluff near Whitesburg on the Chattahoochee, where the park is now.

Senoia's Main Street in earlier days
Photo courtesy of Senoia Area Historical Society

Senoia's earliest automobiles

I recently ran across some kin of Mr. Burnett, who operated the shoe and leather repair shop, and we were discussing old times. They said that Mr. Burnett never owned an auto. If they had to go somewhere out of town, his brother would take them. Years ago, cars were few and traffic was light.

When my mother and dad married in approximately 1912 there were only three cars in Senoia, and Mr. Ralph McKnight, who owned one of those cars, took them from the preacher's house to the train station in Senoia, where they left for their honeymoon in Atlanta.

Dad owned a Maxwell auto around 1929, then a Chevy coupe, and when I was a teenager, a Hudson auto. One night, that Hudson streamed oil all the way from Toccoa to Senoia because the packing had come out of the main bearing. My brother Hugh was driving, and we had to stop and buy oil all the way home after visiting Uncle Elam Addy and his wife, Clara.

During the war, we had a 1939 Chrysler Royal. The first time Dad let me drive it to the movie uptown in Senoia, I backed out of the parking space to go up the hill, and the low gear stripped off. Dad and I both had to walk around trying to locate the gear for a couple of weeks so that we could get the car fixed, as the war was going on and parts and repairs were hard to come by. In 1947, after World War II was over and we had been without a decent auto for years, Dad had accumulated a little money, and he got Doc Tinsley, who was going to the auto auction in Atlanta, to see if he could buy him a car.

Doc bought a practically new 1947 Ford. It was black with venetian blinds in the back window, side spotlights and mirrors, chrome around all the doors, and fog lights on front in addition to the regular lights. When he let me drive it to school, I got the attention of all the girls, as new cars were still scarce in 1947.

In the old days, before the TV show *The Walking Dead* brought in the tourists, most shops would be closed on Sundays, by mid-day on Wednesdays, and by 5 p.m. on all the other days. On weekday mornings, you'd see several older men sitting on the benches outside the Baggarly building, playing checkers or just shooting the breeze, watching everyone who walked into the post office or went to the Farmers and Merchants Bank.

Now we have many shops up and down Main Street, open seven days a week. There are even several shops in the former Hutchinson Hardware building. One of the first businesses to set up shop was Table Talk, owned and managed by retired teacher Jim Preece and his partner, Tony Hinshaw. This store brings in the ladies while the men go to Maguire's Irish Pub or take *Walking Dead* filming location tours. Senoia has more restaurant choices than there are days of the week now.

Above, Ellis Crook with Lynne Fischgrund and below, Jim Barnette,
Mary Welden Brown, Kathryn Callie Welden, Ellis Crook,
and Dorothy Smith Massengale,
Photos courtesy of Senoia Area Historical Society

"How may I direct your call?"

My earliest knowledge of the telephone exchange in Senoia is of Mr. and Mrs. Ludwick operating the switchboard in a small house across from the Hollberg Hotel, now called The Veranda, the big Greek Revival mansion at the corner of Barnes and Seavy Streets. The telephone office was in a small frame house, and the switchboard was located in the front room, facing the street.

Mr. and Mrs. Ludwick were the original operators, as in the beginning, there were very few who could afford this new telephone service. Later, Elna Whitlock Couch, Gladys Attaway Stamps, Ruth Hubbard McDaniel, Jackie Hinesley, and others were the phone drop-cord operators there, and they could listen in on all the phone conversations and knew all the gossip.

If you wanted to find someone in Senoia or needed to get in touch with someone, these ladies knew where they were. They knew who was cheating on whom, as they listened in while connecting the cords and heard all kinds of conversations.

If you heard a siren, you could call the telephone office,

and they knew whose house the ambulance went to. They even knew who was cheating on their wife. Our number was 47-W, the Sewells' residence was 46-J, McKnight Gin was number 8, and later, Crook's Store was 90. It was quite different from today's smartphones.

We were on a party line. If you picked up the phone and the other people were on the line talking, you had to wait until they hung up the receiver to place your call, as some party lines had more than two people on that line. You had one ring or two rings denoting whose phone was being called.

*Mrs. Nellie Addy and her automobile somewhere near Senoia
Photo courtesy of Senoia Area Historical Society, made available by the
late Joanne Utt for a local bank calendar and provided by the
Eastside School project "Stepping Back—Looking Forward."*

The Baggarly Buggy Museum

In the Baggarly Buggy Museum on Main Street sits the Model T that my mother's first cousin Nellie Addy drove, and her picture rests on the fender of the automobile. The fact that a woman drove a car in those days was a novel idea, which is probably why the picture was made. (The Senoia Area Historical Society has a copy, too.) Nellie would drive to Senoia from her dad's farm, probably her furthermost point, as roads were rough or muddy and gas was hard to come by. Only a few places carried gasoline and then only in hand-pumped storage tanks.

Jim Addy, Nellie's father, lived on a one-horse farm on Highway 85 at the corner of Hardy Road and Highway 85 north of Haralson. I remember that the hinges on the barn doors were made of wood, as they could be made on the property. Metal hinges had to be bought. No doubt it was to save travel time and money that they made wooden hinges, as in Mr. Joe Couch's house, he had wooden hinges on doors, with a string hanging out to pull up the wooden stick and open the door.

A "one-horse farm" means only one person plowed a

mule, and everything that was raised or cultivated was done with one person and one mule. They didn't make much money, and they grew everything they ate except salt and sugar and coffee, which they drank very little of.

When the mail was dropped from the trains, Mr. Couch pushed a wheelbarrow containing the mail from the Atlantic Coast Line Railroad Depot all the way up Seavy Street. His wheelbarrow is on display in the Baggarly Museum in Senoia.

Behind the museum is the Senoia water tank. Sometime in the 1950s or maybe later, each Wednesday at noon, the fire siren mounted on the water tank uptown was activated, letting the stores know it was time to close. By the way, the first wooden-body wagon with the fire hoses loaded in it was located in Mr. D. Hunter's barn just back of the three-story building that now houses Maguire's. Later, a small fire truck was located in the building that now houses the Welcome Center. There were no fire hydrants in Senoia until 1937.

Cemeteries in and around Senoia

The Senoia Cemetery Association over the years has done a great job maintaining the primary cemetery in Senoia through donations and investing money and, at one time, drawing good interest on the money. The officers of the association are very civic-minded citizens who live among us and serve with no pay while keeping the grass cut and appearances maintained throughout the cemetery. Among those buried in the Senoia City Cemetery are my parents, Arry Lee Crook (February 19, 1888-January 20, 1980) and Leola Mae Addy (February 27, 1887-December 1, 1973).

In 2009, two teenagers vandalized Tranquil Cemetery and, according to estimates, did $100,000 in damage to tombstones located there, where the first Presbyterian church was founded years ago. This cemetery is located one mile east of Turin.

I received a letter in 2009 from the Coweta County Genealogical Society with the correct information as to the birth and death of my grandparents, John Thomas Addy and R. Florence Morgan Addy and their five-year-old daughter Mamie, who is buried there also. I placed new granite markers on Mamie's and John T. and Florence Morgan Addy's grave sites, as they were not vandalized but getting hard to read.

John Thomas Addy was born April 1, 1860, and died March 2, 1933. R. Florence Morgan Addy was born August 16, 1860, and died February 24, 1902. Daughter Mamie was born December 12, 1897, and died September 27, 1903, at age five.

My mother told me once that her sister Mamie could sing "When the Roll Is Called Up Yonder." I think I shall request that song at my funeral.

Industry comes to Senoia

Southern Mills came to Senoia around 1941. Back then, Parker Cleveland worked on Stewart Avenue for Mr. William (Bill) Ellis, and together with Parker's dad, C. H. Cleveland, and some others, they got seed money to build a plant in Senoia. Mr. Ellis was a true gentleman, and Mr. W. M. Thompson was his superintendent at the Senoia mill (there were five mills at one time, two of which were in Senoia). Southern Mills hosted a meal in the lunchroom at Brantley Institute one night a month followed by singing in the auditorium of the old songs like "Tenting on the Old Campground," "America the Beautiful," "God Bless America," and various pep songs of that nature followed by a speaker. They strived to make this community one you were proud to live in.

I served as president of Senoia Developers, Inc., which was formed to help sell bonds to build the second mill for Southern Mills. After Mr. Bill Ellis' death, his son, Doug Ellis, ran the company before finally selling out to the Dutch company TenCate.

David Johnson, who was from a little town in South Georgia, came to Coweta County and, super salesman that he was, talked Bank of Coweta President Scott Wilson into bankrolling him and built the Flex-On, Inc. plastics plant in Senoia. This plant was operated with great success and expansion. Down the road, Flex-on sold out to Winpak, which has expanded with another plant across from the original buildings.

The property that Flex-On originally started to build on was the City of Senoia trash dump, where garbageman Hubert Hunt piled the city's garbage and burned it in those days. (Hubert was a great source of information. When I wanted to know what kind of alcohol someone drank, or if they did, I simply asked him, as he could report based on his collections of the trash.)

When David sought the loan after having bought the property from the city and the title was run, someone who was (no doubt) hoping to stop the use of the property alleged that hazardous materials were on the site. David managed to get a sworn statement by the overall-wearing mayor stating that no hazardous waste had ever been placed upon this property.

Bobbie Blandenburg is elected

Bobbie Middlebrooks Blandenburg was the first black person to serve on the Senoia City Council. She had worked in bookkeeping at Coweta-Fayette Electric Membership Corporation and, with her experience, opened her own bookkeeping service in Senoia on Bridge Street. She was the daughter of Robert (Bob) and Lizzie Middlebrooks, who farmed on Chestlehurst Road. They were a hardworking middle-class family, and in addition to Bobbie, their other children were Jessie, Naomi, Harvey, and Marvin.

Jessie lived in Tennessee and worked for a Mrs. Kinser, making pimiento cheese and chicken salad for Mrs. Kinser's lady friends and party friends to enjoy. Because of this good food Jessie cooked, Mrs. Kinser's Salads, A Southern Salad Tradition was begun. Jessie went from plant to plant and was in charge of quality control as well as labor relations for the company.

During the Depression years of 1930-31, Bob Middlebrooks went to his smokehouse and took meat—and, no doubt, canned garden products—and gave them to a white family whose head of the family was absent or dead, as the children needed food, and there was no social security or welfare in those days. A descendant of this white family later became a mayor of Senoia.

Will Horton's store

Around 1915, Mr. Will Horton ran a small store near the intersection of Highway 85 and Dolly Nixon Road. There was not enough business for some reason, and it was closed down. He came to Senoia and operated a cottonseed-oil processing plant adjacent to Daniel's Gin, where the Senoia post office is now located, at the intersection of Broad Street and Gin Street. Just behind Daniel's Gin was McKnight's Gin, owned by P. R. McKnight and operated by Mr. Claude Johnson, a man of high integrity whom the farmers entrusted with their samples and grading of their cotton. He stored the cotton in warehouses on his property while the cotton was awaiting sale. Mr. Claude's daughter, Louise Johnson Atkinson, to my memory was the first woman city clerk. Mr. J. B. Hutchinson was the city clerk before then, and there was very little money to administer. The books were nothing at all compared to modern times. The city had no tractors or earth-moving equipment, and there was just one old truck for Hubert to pick up the garbage in, and there was only a small amount of garbage in those days.

Second location of the Senoia Library
Photo courtesy of the Senoia Area Historical Society

Joanne Utt and the Senoia Library

Joanne and Charles (Chuck) Utt moved to Senoia around the early 1970s, and Joanne established the Senoia Library. She worked with no remuneration for years before the library became more fully funded and had paid staff. Joanne was also instrumental in getting all the shrubbery planted in downtown Senoia as well as getting the Senoia Historic District on the National Register of Historic Places.

Descendants of the original settlers never realized what a historical treasure we had, as some never traveled to distant lands so they could come back with a greater appreciation of our heritage and location.

Ellis Crook with the turkey he cooked for
Thanksgiving in 2017
Photo courtesy of the Crook family

Senoia's first sawmiller

Dad built his own barns and sheds. You went to the sawmill, hauled the lumber back, and used flat rocks as pillars. There were no permits or architects or building fees. The average house was built by homebuilders with no plans, only their ingenuity and brainpower used to design as they went along.

The first sawmiller in Senoia was Mr. Andrew Nations, who owned quite a bit of land on Seavy Street. Then Grady Pate had a good-size sawmill where Clark Street goes across on the south side of Highway 16. H. L. Pollard came out of Fayette County, worked at Southern Mills, then got into the sawmill business and did super. His descendants live here—Sonny Pollard and his wife, Vickie Williams Pollard, and Becky Pollard Bell and her husband, Jon.

Years ago, they burned the slabs or bark side of the cut tree, as there was no market for slab lumber. As time went along, every bit of the wood was utilized in some manner. Now the big experiment is using the pellets or the utility part of the wood to generate electricity.

My mother told me that Mr. Allen Jones operated the first

Delco-battery-stored electricity for Senoia and that it only lasted a few hours each night. Mr. Allen Jones also walked each weekday to Starr's Mill, where he operated a cotton gin on one side of the dam and a gristmill on the opposite side.

Before he died in the 1920s, Will Horton operated the cottonseed-oil processing plant next to Daniel's Gin, both of which were where the Senoia post office is now located. His widow, Alice P. Horton, lived in a small house behind what now is Synovus (formerly Bank of Coweta), and the house still stands at the corner of Crook Street and Luther Bailey Road. There were no Social Security checks during her lifetime, and she sewed and rented out three rooms on the north side of her house to Frank and Georgene Harris for a number of years. She had the only well during those times that was a bored well, and it was under a shed roof attached to the house. The cylinder bucket was only about six inches in diameter. In the bottom of the bucket was a plunger that pushed up when the bucket hit the water, and it let the water flow in from the bottom of the bucket. After letting the bucket sit for a minute or so, you then drew on the rope. As you pulled up on the bucket, the plunger hole in the bottom would drop into a closed position, and you brought up a full cylinder of water. The last bucket of this type was in Hutchinson Hardware in Senoia prior to the sale of the building. Now, with bored wells, you merely drop the pump down and electrically pump the water. Mrs. Horton, whom

I knew as Hoyt, grew a large garden, and her two siblings were Mozelle Horton Young and Paul Horton.

Mozelle taught music in Atlanta, and Paul traveled for a snuff and tobacco company. He settled in Little Rock, Arkansas, where one of his sons, Clyde Horton, was the famous football coach of Little Rock High School who worked through all the integration problems at Little Rock. He was still helping coach in his seventies.

Mr. Allen Jones and Mr. Walt Arnall each had a plaque in the sanctuary of the First Baptist Church of Senoia. It was propped on molding to the left of the pulpit, but as time marched on and nobody remembered them, the plaques were removed.

Similarly, Mr. Bob Walt Freeman's picture hung in the bank on Highway 16 East—formerly Farmers and Merchants Bank, later First Choice, and now Bank OZK. This picture hung in the lobby, was later removed to the back offices, and I doubt it exists now, as he had no grandchildren or survivors to check on it periodically. Let's see how long the picture of Mrs. Hazel (Walt) Thompson hangs in the Bank of Coweta (Synovus in 2019). She had originally worked for Farmers and Merchants Bank but left when Bank of Coweta President Scott Wilson saw her potential and made her an offer to set up and manage a branch here in Senoia. She is a lovely lady, always well-dressed and with perfect hair, and she represented the bank well.

Ellis Crook horseback-riding in Senoia
Photo courtesy of the Crook family

The Culpeppers and other families

Dr. Wilbur F. Culpepper had two daughters. Edith married a lawyer named Turpin and lived in Macon. The other daughter, Mary, bless her soul, did not have a model physique, and one of her eyes was distorted, but she operated the first lunchroom at Brantley Institute in Senoia. The Culpepper house at the corner of Morgan Street and Broad Street was built by Dr. John Addy.

The government back then issued surplus food to the school, and pork and beans was the mainstay. Miss Culpepper would put bacon on top, season the beans with honey, and try different methods of serving them, but it was still pork and beans.

When I was nine or ten, I arrived early at school and built a fire in the lunchroom stove, and for that, I got a free lunch. I was born way too soon to get a free lunch without working.

Directly across the street from the Culpepper house lived the old maid Sims sisters—Miss Nan, Miss Jimma, and Miss Sack, who ran the millinery store uptown below where the Masonic Hall is now. Miss Nan Sims was a staunch—and expressive—member of Senoia United Methodist Church. A lady of some size, she made—and wore—large hats.

Mr. William James "Nat" Estes, the grandfather of Diane Estes and Eleanor Estes Wilkinson, had one son, William Jr. (Bill) Estes, and several daughters. One daughter, Ruth, lived with the old maids, and another, Mary Claude, could have lived there part-time.

Ruth Estes married Render Gresham, and she traveled with Render in his sales job, as they took me out to dinner in Columbia, South Carolina, around 1952. I had to buy three parcels of land to build Crook's Supermarket—one from Render Gresham after Ruth died, one from Dr. Charles Daniel's widow, and an access lot to Morgan Street from the Doc Tinsley heirs. With the new shops and overhead condos, the Morgan Street property gives customers supermarket access whether they arrive at the back of the store by walking or by golf cart.

I couldn't have imagined having a golf cart when I was a boy. At the beginning of World War II, I got a rebuilt second-hand bicycle, and I thought that was great. I had a one-horse wagon that I hitched a mule to and traveled around town, one time to Haralson and back with, of course, some girls on the wagon. We stopped on the way to Haralson and put a watermelon in the branch to cool. On the way back, we stopped and cut the watermelon and enjoyed a good time. The branch was located on Dolly Nixon Road in the days before Georgia 85 was built. I painted on the wagon body "HI,

GIRLIE," "TAXI," "SAVE GAS," and various other slogans, as World War II was going on and gas was rationed. The price with Office of Price Administration (OPA) stamps was five gallons for ninety cents. Bootlegged gas was fifty cents a gallon if you did not have ration stamps, but just think, you could buy a Coke for five cents and an ice cream hunkie for five cents back then.

Cokes were allotted, and we got a couple of cases a week and hid them behind the ice in the outside ice storage box for regular customers and a Baptist preacher's wife who flirted with Dad. I dated her daughters.

Back in the days before refrigeration, in the 1920s and early 1930s, people who had the pasture space would raise a calf to a considerable size, and they and three other people would also be raising what we called a "beef," and they formed a beef club. They would join up to slaughter one of the beefs at one member's place, and you got one fourth of that beef to take home with you. You would get a front quarter of the cow one time and a hindquarter the next time. You got roasts and ground beef one time and steak and ground beef the next time. These events occurred during cold weather so that they could be held in the barn of a building outdoors to keep the meat cold.

Crook's Marketplace as it is today
Photo courtesty the Crook family

Ellis Crook from a 2016 feature in Newnan-Coweta Magazine
Photo courtesy of Mark Fritz Photography

Our service with the grocery co-op

A co-op, when run properly, gives you a competitive edge, as the object is to sell to the store at an upcharge that covers only the expense of operating the warehouse and getting the merchandise to the store at the lowest possible price. Years ago, we mailed in our order listing the amount of each item needed next to each IBM ordering number. Today, a machine can scan the shelf tag and order several hundred cases in a matter of seconds. The goods come in with the shelf tag number on the case, and twice a week, shelf tags come in with the latest retail price to be downloaded into the computer and tags hung in front of the product.

It's a great operation, but we don't have time to sit down and enjoy tales around the potbellied stove as in years gone by. To be competitive, "service" is the name of the game along with taking care of the customer's needs.

In September of 1959, we first joined a co-op, Associated Grocers Co-op of Atlanta, from which we as a stock owner purchased our groceries, meats, and other provisions. My brother Alva L. Crook was serving on the board of directors at that time. After his departure from the board, I served for a number of years prior to its demise. I later joined Associated Grocers Co-op of Alabama in Birmingham. My son Greg served on its board from the time he was twenty-seven, making him one of its youngest board members ever. He served for twenty-eight years until we changed co-ops, elected by fellow grocers in five states each time his term came up for re-election. Those were a lot of trips to Birmingham. We now belong to a national co-op representing some four thousand chain stores.

In August of 1981, we opened the first supermarket that Senoia ever had, and it was an experience after running a small gas station/grocery combo. I compared it to driving a small auto and then flying a jumbo jet, and I wanted to go back to the gas station. But after having borrowed around six hundred thousand dollars, I had no choice but to work twelve-hour days and sweat the checkbook.

We had paper food coupons issued by the government, and due to some people getting them unscrupulously and selling them in exchange for money to buy alcohol or tobacco, the government has in the last few years given people a credit card called an EBT card. Each month, it is loaded with the amount of money the government allocates to them for food. Items in the store are scanned with the UPC code, and only food may be paid for with this card.

Nonedible items are not available to EBT cardholders, as they have to personally pay for anything they cannot consume. No drugs, paper goods, dog and cat food, or alcoholic goods may be obtained with these cards. The user has a secret five-digit number they have to punch after scanning their card, and this allows for the money transfer.

Ellis Crook and family decorating their Christmas tree
Photo courtesy of the Crook family

Christmastime of the 1930s

In the 1930s at Christmastime, the merchants on Main Street put glass showcases on the sidewalk in front of their stores, and school-age personnel sold firecrackers, candy, and various small articles from these showcases. The wagons and mules or horses were tied out back of the stores because of the noise and people on this gala pre-Christmas Day. In the fall, when cotton was being ginned at Daniel's or McKnight's gin, more money was being spent than at any other time of the year as farmers and sharecroppers were being paid for their cotton.

What we called sharecropping was a deal in which the landlord furnishes the land, seed, fertilizer, and mules or tractors, and the person doing the work is paid one-half of the proceeds of the harvest, and with no irrigation, this is a huge gamble. Some landowners were deceitful in their relationship with the sharecroppers, charging them a large percentage on the money advanced them during the growing season for them to live on and buy such essentials as sugar and salt. If they did not raise enough hogs, chickens, and a large garden, they had a hard time surviving, as there was no money to go to the store as weekly wage earners do in these more modern times.

They usually had no automobiles, no insurance, no water bill—a well furnished their water—and only a little kerosene for lamps. Later, REA electrical co-op came through the country. Sharecroppers paid no taxes. Sometimes, unscrupulous landowners would let them plant and cultivate the crop, keep out the grass by plowing, then poison the cotton with arsenic powder (to kill the weevils) by using blowers either on their back or a mule-pulled blower. Then the unethical landowner would make them move and not pay them their share of the value of the crop but would hire someone else to gather it in the fall. Of course, some had borrowed too much against their crop and did not receive what they thought was due them.

This was the time of year that C. P. Daniel and the owner of Hollberg's came up with the idea of giving away tickets on merchandise bought from them and having a big joint drawing for money on Saturday afternoon. They had greased pole climbing, and for prizes, they threw turkeys from the top of buildings. They put on quite a gathering to bring people to town and ring up sales while the money from cotton sales was prevalent.

The first time I rode the cotton-filled wagon to the gin and watched the big suction pipe suck the cotton from the wagon was an experience. The operator of McKnight's Gin was highly respected by the farmers for being fair in grading of their cotton, as some grades were fair or middlin', and the higher the grade, quality-wise, the more money the cotton sold for. The operator was Claude Johnson, whose daughter Louise was one of Senoia's first city clerks years later and justice of the peace. Louise married Joe Atkinson, a retired Senoian who was a colonel in the Marines and whose father, Hubert Atkinson, had a mule collar business in Senoia. The name, I believe, was a Lankford mule collar, and I later learned that Bobby Shell of Clark Street has in his possession one of these collars that is in mint condition.

After a trip out west, Mr. Hubert was able to send his son Joe to Georgia Tech, and Joe remained a staunch Yellow Jacket the rest of his life. One daughter, Edith, married Bill Rowe, who had a joint venture in peach orchards with Mr. Carl McKnight, brother of Paul McKnight Sr. The orchards were on Rock House Road, about three miles out, and there was a rock house across the road from the peach-packing shed. This was across the road from what is now Butcher's Dairy.

Mr. Emmett Freeman, whom I have mentioned before, was a bachelor who lived in a small cabin at the head of Hutchinson Lake, the source of Senoia's water. He had a black beard, wore rubber boots most of the time, and looked like a hermit, but he was sharp with numbers. The tale goes that when the books at Farmers and Merchants Bank were out of balance, Emmett's brother, Bob Walt Freeman, cashier and later president, would bring him into town late in the evening while the bank was closed, and Mr. Emmett would correct and balance the books of the bank, as Mr. Bob Walt didn't want anyone to see his brother because of the way he dressed.

Miss Hattie Shell was head cashier of the bank around 1960 when my wife, Pat, had her doctor perform a small out-patient type operation. On the payment check, I wrote, "for the latest carving." Miss Hattie watched all checks and knew everybody's business in those days, and so the next Sunday, Miss Hattie asked Pat what kind of carving she'd had done. Miss Hattie also kept the books for Senoia Insurance Company, the first insurance company in Senoia, of which Mr. Bob Walt Freeman was owner.

Before the Depression, there were three banks in Senoia, which was a thriving business town. One of them was Redwine Bank out of Fayetteville, and the others were First National and Farmers and Merchants. Farmers and Merchants was the survivor of the three due to the fact that, as everyone was taking their money out of the banks, Mr. Bob Walt Freeman (or Mr. Luther Hardy) thought up the idea of putting a basket full of dollar bills inside the pay window, where people taking their money out could see that the bank had money.

By that afternoon or the next day, people started putting their money back into the bank. That was a smart public relations move that saved the bank. And all to say that around 2009, the Farmers and Merchants Bank was sold. Directors of the new bank borrowed the money for real estate purchases and lost the bank to the FDIC, who sold it to Bank of Ozark. Quite a few Senoians lost a chunk of money, as they had stock in this bank at that time, as the common stock was the only kind of stock that went down the gutter. As all living during this era know, a lot of banks folded at this time, and earnings were nonexistent. I learned from my brother-in-law Ray Sewell that the only time you make money in bank stock is when the bank is sold.

Boy Scout recognition at Senoia United Methodist Church in 2018
Photo courtesy of the Senoia UMC

Scouting in Senoia

In the history of Senoia, I dare not forget to mention Billy Adcock, the most devoted Boy Scout leader who ever presided over Troop 49 in Senoia. Billy reorganized or re-chartered Troop 49 in 1967 and remained Scoutmaster for thirty years, when he had to step down due to ill health. Billy Adcock had only one daughter, Kim, and later a granddaughter, Jenna, but he had several thousand "sons" that he guided through scouting. Quite a group of them made Eagle Scout, and some of his scouts attended the National Jamboree in Pennsylvania in 1977. Billy also served as chairman of the St. Jude Bike-A-Thon, which was very successful and raised quite a sum of money for a worthy cause.

Billy grew up in the school of hard knocks, and therefore he understood situations some boys were having in trying to play ball and attend scout meetings. He hauled them to ball practice and later home, and he used his own money to pay for supplies used in scouting. He was not a selfish man and *Newnan Times Herald* columnist Johnny Brown once praised him in a newspaper article for his selflessness. Billy always went about his civic duties in a quiet and unassuming manner. He was known as "Mr. Billy" all over the eastern side of the county.

Billy became president of the East Coweta Little League in 1978 and served for fourteen years as president, one year as vice president, and one year as treasurer. In 1977, he received the Distinguished Service Award. He was presented the Silver Beaver Award for scouting in 1979, and in 1984, he was presented the East Coweta Little League and Community Award.

When he became president of the Little League, games were held behind what is now East Coweta Middle School. Later, after the Leroy Johnson Park was built near Winpak Films in Senoia, the games were relocated there, and the senior field was named and dedicated to Billy.

Joining Billy in leadership was Virgil Brooks, who has freely given of his time with Boy Scout Troop 49 for forty-three years. Virgil's sons, Robin and Emmanuel, and his nephew, Edward Brooks, all ranked high in scouting, and several of them made Eagle Scout.

Then along came another dedicated soul, Glen Roberts, who is a master electrician by trade and has worked with Troop 49 for twenty-five years. Also, Tommy Smith for fifteen years has given all of his free time and talent in serving the boys of this area in all aspects of scouting.

I was a Boy Scout in Troop 49 around 1946, and we did not have the leadership that this troop has enjoyed since Billy

Adcock re-chartered the troop in the spring of 1967 and led it until his health failed him. Senoia and this area have been blessed with great leadership for quite a number of years in the field of scouting.

Pat and Ellis Crook in 1983
Photo courtesy of the Crook family

My wife, Pat

As an addendum to all my previous writings about Senoia and my family history, I find myself remiss in not having mentioned my greatest asset that helped all this happen. She was my wife—Ardith Patricia Yarbrough Crook, the only child of Hubert G. and Mary Williams Yarbrough of the Beulah community in Lee County, Alabama. She came to this part of the country (Newnan) after graduating from Alabama Polytechnic Institute (now Auburn University) to teach Home Economics at East Coweta High School. We met in 1956 at a school dance, she as the teacher coordinating the student participation and I as a chaperon for my nieces Carol Ann and Arleen, who attended school then. I courted her by sending her small treats (like apples and candy bars) with the school food orders for her Home Economics classes. I am sure some of the girls she taught encouraged the courtship.

We married on July 10, 1960 and had three children, Cheryl Denise Crook (Thompson), Kenneth Hubert Crook, and Gregory Ellis Crook. Ken was murdered on September 30, 2005, by a robber seeking money from the Tire Center (which Ken operated). The man who did this was convicted and has since died in prison.

I bought my dad's inventory in January 1960 and paid him each week on that purchase of fifteen thousand dollars. Because I had a vacant cinder block building up the street, I later got into the tire business and started selling one or two at a time, building the business slowly. Then, I started a small loan business due to people needing a few dollars or needing to pay for groceries on the weekend when they got paid. Today we have Crook's, Inc. (two supermarkets—one in Newnan), Crook's Super Corporation (a convenience store and eight-bay gas station), Crook's Tire Center, McIntosh Finance Company, and in addition to my and Greg's companies, he has Crescent South Insurance Company.

All that is to say that I can look up the street and see the land on which I picked 125 pounds of cotton one afternoon, and one mile down the road, I can see where I lived and planted cotton with a mule and cotton planter when I was nine years old.

I appreciate the great life I have lived and my great heritage.

THE END

Ellis Crook is honored at a Roast at Founders
Restaurant in Senoia.
Photo courtesy of Hal Sewell

Leola Mae Addy Crook and Arry Lee Crook
Photo courtesy of the Crook family

Appendix

Ellis Crook's parents and siblings

Ellis' father, Arry Lee Crook, was born February 19, 1888 and died on January 20, 1980. He worked hard all through his life and had good times and some not-so-good times. In reality, he had some very difficult times.

Ellis' mother, Leola Mae Addy, was born February 27, 1887, and died December 1, 1973. She married Arry Lee Crook on December 15, 1912. She was a sweet lady, a wonderful cook, and she helped to keep the family together.

Arry Lee and Leola Crook had 4 sons and 1 daughter:
1. Julian Lee Crook, born October 18, 1913; married Laura Walton.
2. Florence Edith Crook, born April 20, 1915; married Ray Shelnutt Sewell, August 13, 1936.
3. Alva Lee Crook, born January 11, 1917; married Miriam Lester September 6, 1940.
4. Hugh Dorsey Crook, born January 21, 1919, died July 31, 1964; married Phyllis Byrnes, May 1, 1945.
5. Wilbur Ellis Crook, born June 1, 1931; married Patricia Yarbrough on July 10, 1960.

Over the years, Ellis and Pat had 3 children: Cheryl, Greg, and Ken. Unfortunately, they lost Ken several years ago in a senseless act of violence.

Crook ancestors

Ellis Crook's paternal grandparents' info:

Ozwell Crook born February 16, 1861, died June 18, 1922. He married Jennie Pattilo Higgins, born July 14, 1862, died March 17, 1956. They were married December 27, 1882. They are buried in the Senoia City Cemetery, Coweta County, Georgia. They had 11 children: 3 sons—including Arry Lee Crook, Ellis' father—and 8 daughters.

Ellis Crook's paternal great-grandparents' info:

Louelen Crook was born, September 26, 1827, and died August 18, 1901. Louelen is shown in the 1830 Douglas County, Georgia census in the community of Fairplay. He lived in Carroll County in 1860 but was employed as a farmer in Coweta County in the 1870 census, most likely making him the first member of this Crook family to live in Coweta County. In 1880 Louelen and family had moved to Meriwether County, returning to Coweta by 1900. Louelen married Sarah E. Pennington, born June 26, 1837, and died on August 14, 1917. She was the daughter of William Henry and Mary Elizabeth Coggin Pennington.

Louelen joined the Confederate Army on March 10, 1862. He was a Private in Company C, 35th Regiment, Campbell County, known as the "Campbell Rangers." He was wounded and admitted to the 1st Georgia Hospital on June 27, 1862. He was transferred to 'Hanlietere's Co.' of Joe Thompson's Georgia Artillery, as a Private, on February 9, 1863. He is listed as deserting this unit on January 11, 1864.

He returned to the 35th Regiment, Company C, and was captured at Petersburg, Virginia, April 2, 1865. Louelen was released at Hart's Island, New York, June 15, 1865 after spending only 2 months as a POW. Louelen and his wife Sarah applied for Confederate Pensions in Coweta County,

Georgia, listing his service in the Artillery Unit.

Louelen and Sarah E. Crook are buried in the cemetery of the former Bethel Methodist Church on Luther Bailey Road in Senoia, Coweta County, Georgia. They had 8 children: 5 sons and 3 daughters.

Ellis Crook's paternal great-great-grandparents' info:

Griffin Crook was born about 1794 in Virginia. His family moved to North Carolina where Griffin married Nancy Pennington, March 18, 1817, in Wake County, North Carolina. She was born about 1800 in Virginia, the daughter of Howell and Margaret Pennington.

Griffin and family moved to Pike County, Georgia by 1830, Meriwether County by 1840, and was employed as a Farmer in Spalding County, 2nd District in the 1860 Census.

Addy ancestors

Ellis Crook's maternal grandparents' info:

Although not as detailed at this point as the Crook ancestry, the Addy genealogy also consists of many levels.

Ellis' grandfather was John Thomas Addy. He was married twice. He had eight children with first wife Ruth Florence (Morgan) Addy, including Leola Mae Addy, Ellis' mother. John and his second wife, Mary (Haines) Addy had one daughter.

John Addy and his brother, Alfred Addy, bought and farmed 100 acres of land adjacent to each other. The property was about 3 miles outside of Senoia, off Standing Rock Road. Furthermore, these brothers (John and Alfred) married two sisters from the Morgan family.

The children of these two unions were considered to be double first cousins. Among the children of Alfred and his wife were Kate and Isadore Addy who were "famous" for the hot dogs they served for many years from their store in downtown Senoia.

Ellis' grandmother, Florence Morgan Crook, was from the Morgan settlers who migrated from Newberry County, South Carolina to the Senoia, Coweta County area around 1827.

Daniel Morgan, along with his wife Mary Lankford and two brothers, Ezekiel and William (Billie), moved to Coweta County from Newberry, South Carolina where they were born. Ezekiel is buried in the Elmore cemetery in Senoia, according to oral history.

The Georgia Land Lottery in 1827 resulted from the 1825 Indian Springs Treaty that was signed, among others, by William McIntosh who was a Chief of the Lower Creek Indians. When land opened up with the lottery, LOTS of people suddenly were interested in Georgia including many different families in Newberry County, South Carolina. Included among these families were the Addys, the Morgans, and the Shells.

Florence Morgan Addy Crook died on February 24, 1902. There was ice hanging from all the trees, and her children could not attend the burial. John Thomas Addy died on March 3, 1933. They lived on what is now Bell Spring Road. They were originally of the Baptist faith, but due to inclement weather one year, they could not attend in their horse and buggy for a month or more. When they ultimately arrived at their church in Senoia one Sunday, some narrow-minded person would not serve them sacrament. Therefore on the way home, John said to Florence, "I guess we will join the Methodist church," which was within one mile from their home. Although the Standing Rock Methodist Church no longer exists, local descendants continue to worship at the Methodist church in Senoia.

Ellis Crook's maternal great-grandparents' info:

John Addy was the son of William Harrison Addy and Mary Susan (Hunter) Addy.

Ellis Crook's maternal great-great-grandparents' info:

Harrison Addy was the son of Jessie Addy by his first wife, Mary Summer. Mary died when Jessie was approximately 42 years of age, leaving five children of maturing age, one of whom later became a doctor in Senoia.

After Mary's death, Jessie married Rachel Haynes, a teenager for a bride/companion. However, his children did not approve since Jessie was 26 years older than Rachel.

Therefore in 1875, he hitched up his mules and wagon and joined a wagon train to Texas. He and Rachel moved to Grayson County near the town of Dennison, Texas.

In 1883, they moved to Gonzales County and settled in Leesville, Texas, where he and Rachel reared another family and he led a most respectful life as a farmer and a member of the Masonic Lodge.

Jessie and Rachel are buried in their daughter's plot (Williams) behind the two churches that off the main road through Leesville, Texas.

The only child of five that Jessie left behind in Senoia he saw again was Dr. Addy who traveled by train to see his father on his death bed.

Ellis Crook's maternal great-great-great-grandparents' info:

Ellis' great-great-great grandparents were John Simeon Addy, Sr. and his wife Catherine Taylor Addy who were the parents of Jessie Addy.

John Simeon Addy, Sr, was born January 9, 1779, in Lexington County, South Carolina and was married about 1804 to Catherine Taylor. Catherine was born on May 17,

1789, and died February 16, 1857.

Both John and Catherine are buried on the William Lloyd Addy Farm in Lexington County. To their union was born 12 children (8 sons and 4 daughters), some of whom remained in South Carolina and some who moved to other states.

Made in the USA
Columbia, SC
05 May 2022

59970031R00093